Poems

Quotes

&

THOUGHTS PROVOKED

NIMA

POEMS, QUOTES & THOUGHTS PROVOKED

COPYRIGHT ©2014 Carletta Pickett

Printed in the United States of America

ISBN-13:978-0692331965
ISBN-10:0692331964

Printed by Createspace in 2014
Printed by BlaqRayn Publishing Plus in 2014

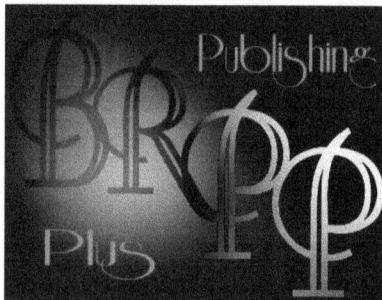

Dedication

TAKING TIME TO THANK THE MOST HIGH
FOR ALL BLESSINGS
TO MY FAMILY...WHAT CAN I SAY TO MAKE
YOU UNDERSTAND? I LOVE YOU! I
APPRECIATE THE HELP, SUPPORT AND
UNDERSTANDING THAT YOU GIVE ME EACH
DAY. WHERE WOULD I BE WITHOUT YOU?
SEE YOU WHEN I GET HOME.
EXTENDED FAMILY AND FRIENDS
THANK YOU MS. CYNTHIA
THANKS FOR THE HELP MY POETIC PEEPS
FAMILY POETRY COLLECTIVE (PHILLY)
THANK YOU FOR THE SUPPORT AND A
FORMAT TO SHINE.
SPARK....RUQUE.....CONSCIOUS...
THANK YOU FOR THE EXTRA SUPPORT AND
JUMPING IN. FAMILY FOR LIFE
FINALLY SHERRICE JONES...BORN FREE...KIM
MORROW, YOU THREE HAVE TAKEN MY
DREAMS AND ALLOWED THEM TO TAKE
FLIGHT...
YOU GUYS HAVE STARTED A MOVEMENT I
IT'S JUST GETTING STARTED....
MAD LOVE

NIMA

Poems

Quotes

&

THOUGHTS PROVOKED

NIMA

Chapter 1

NOTICE ME

NOTICE ME NOTICING YOU
FEEL MY ENERGY FROM ACROSS THE ROOM HEAR
MY VOICE THOUGH I SING NO SONG TAKE MY
HAND EVEN IF IT'S FOR A SECOND I DON'T THINK
ANYONE WILL DETECT IT WRITE A POEM AND
DEDICATE IT TO ME
USE HER NAME INSTEAD OF MINE FOR OTHERS TO
SEE
BUT JUST BENEATH THE SURFACE
THERE IS AN UNDER TONE
A SMALL MOAN
YOU CALLING FOR ME
BECAUSE YOU CAN'T LEAVE ME ALONE
DISTANCE IS JUST A MATTER OF SPACE
CONTROVERSY IS HER MIDDLE NAME SO SHE
SOMETIMES FORGETS THE FIRST
POETRY THAT SHIT
HIS WORDS BE HER TWIST
SERVED HOT AND SMOOTH IS THAT PERFECT DISH

THE MAN IS

HE IS ROUGH AND SMOOTH

GOOD AND BAD
COMMANDS RESPECT WITHOUT SAYING A WORD
BAD BOY TURNED GOOD BECAME A MAN
NOT TOO MANY CAN UNDERSTAND
CRAZY SEXY COOL AND NOT FROM, THE GROUP
BUT IF HE HAD ONE I WOULD CALL THEM THE
STALLIONS

SENSITIVE BUT AT TIMES COULD GIVE A FUCK
IN HIS ARMS FEELING SAFE AND SECURE
SEX IS OUT OF THIS WORLD
LOVE BEING BLACK
LOVE HIS PEEPS

SO DON'T LET HIM HAVE TO RETURN TO THE
HEAT FUCK WITH HIM BEWARE OF THE
AFTERMATH LINE UP YOUR BOYS IT MAY BE A
BLOODBATH PROMOTING PEACE HE WANTS TO BE
ABOUT NIGGA WANT TO TEST HIM

BRING EM OUT BRING EM OUT

DON'T GET THAT MAN STARTED OR SOME MAY BE
DEARLY DEPARTED
MY WORDS MAY OFFEND SOME
BUT I KNOW WH3ERE HE CAME FROM
SAW HIM FROM ACROSS THE ROOM
HE WOULD BE MY PENDING DOOM
EVERY INCH OF HIM IS TUCKED AWAY IN MY
HEART

So that means he and I will never part
Blue skies or illusions there of His dick
fits me like a glove Because he is...THE MAN

MAYBE

*THOUGHTS OF ME MAY ENTER HIS MIND AND I
WILL NEVER KNOW*

JUST MAYBE HE WILL MISS THESE LIPS

*WILL HE TAKE A MINUTE TO REWIND AND DAZE
UPON A TIME? WHEN WE COULD EAT AND SLEEP
US
EGO CRASHING TO THE GROUND*

IT LIFTED US FROM THE GROUND

*AND WE WATCHED THOSE BELOW ENVY US
BECAUSE THEY COULDN'T UNDERSTAND THE
CONNECTION OF US*

*FRAGMENTS OF A RELATIONSHIP IS WHAT WE HAD
PORTIONS OF FANTASIES BECAUSE I NEVER REALLY
HAD YOU YOU UNCONCERNED COMPLETELY HAD
ME
WISH I COULD PRESS REWIND OR HAVE AN
ALTERNATE ENDING*

ALL I KNOW IS LOVE

I WANT TO SAY SOMETHING WITTY
I WANT TO PUT TWO FINGERS IN THE AIR AND
REPRESENT MY CITY
BUT ALL I KNOW IS LOVE
I WISH I COULD BE POLITICAL RIGHT NOW
I WISH I COULD GET DOWN WITH MY PROFOUND
I WANT TO TALK RELIGION AND SPIRITUALITY BUT
IN FACT IN ALL REALITY.. I BEEN HURT BEEN
CRUSHED
DISAPPEARED FROM MY LIFE LIKE THE MAYANS
DROPPED ME FROM 40,000 FEET IN THE AIR NO
PARACHUTE AND I'M STILL FLYING
I WANT TO BE LOUD AND ANGRY
ALL I WANT TO DO IS WRAP YOU UP IN 6OR7
JOE LOVE SONGS AND GET TO STROKING

Loving The Mornings

It's raining
He loves my hotcakes I love his sausage
Breakfast in Bed
Don't forget the honey
Juice drips
He loves my melons Sticky situations Head
to toe
Oh-My-God...Here he cums

(Subliminally speaking)

BREAKFAST IN BED

THE SUN HAS BEGUN TO RISE AS YOU DO
NO SURPRISE TO ME THAT YOU HAVE A HUNGER
I HAVE AMPLE SERVINGS
LITTLE NIBBLES TURN INTO MAN SIZE BITES COCOA
NEEDS CREAM IF YOU ARE THIRSTY CINNAMON
BUNS WAITING TO BE GLAZED YOU LOVE HOW
THEY GLISTEN
WE SIP AND DRINK IN A PASSIONATE FASHION
WE ARE IN A DELICIOUS STATE OF BEING MELONS
RIPE AND JUICY
MEAT TENDER YET FIRM
I DRINK YOU IN
AFTER BREAKFAST WE BOTH LOOK FORWARD TO
LUNCH

IT'S AFTER MIDNIGHT

WHAT DO I DO WITH YOU NOW? THOUGHTS RUN
THROUGH MY MIND DESIRES TICKLE MY TONGUE
I KNOW WHERE THIS WILL END JUST US HAVING
SOME FUN EXPLORING ONE ANOTHER HOLDING
TOUCHING FEELING EXPLODING
A SEXUALLY CHARGED RACE TO THE FINISH LINE
WE SPEED UP
WE TAKE OUR TIME OPEN MOUTH KISSES
TONGUES DANCE FOR DEAR LIFE PULL ME IN
EVERY TIME
SEDUCTIVE SIPS OF YOU I TAKE IN
UNTIL MY THIRST IS GONE
WAITING AGAIN FOR AFTER MIDNIGHT TO RETURN

LOVE

I AM IN LOVE WITH HIS WORDS
HE SEDUCES ME WITH PHRASES, VERSES,
METAPHORS AND INTELLECTUAL CONVERSATION
SOMETHING SERIOUSLY SEXY ABOUT HIM
THIS SHIT IS DEEP
I FEEL HIM IN MY SLEEP
HIS WORDS HOW THEY CREEP
INTO MY BLOODSTREAM IT GOES
I WAIT FOR HIM IN THE CORNER OF OUR WORLD
HIS WORDS FLOW LIKE THE RIVER AS HE INVITES
MY RIVER TO DO THE SAME

UNTIL MORNING

MY LIPS AND YOUR HIPS
THEY DO INVADE SPACES AND DELIGHT THE
SENSES

ONE TOUCH AND I BEGAN TO BREATHE WITH
EXCITEMENT

THE SOFT KISS AS IF YOUR ARE AFRAID SO SEXY
AND EROTIC

MY CLOTHES FALL TO THE FLOOR

I CAN'T GET YOURS OFF FAST ENOUGH
I WANT IT SO BAD YET I TRY TO RETREAT WHEN
YOU ENTER

PULLING ME DOWN TO YOU
I AM LOST AND FOCUS IS NOT AN OPTION

YOUR FINGERS IN M MOUTH TO KEEP THE NOISE
TO A MINIMUM

LONG HARD STROKES ARE WHAT I'M AFTER MY
BEDROOM IS LIKE A NATURAL DISASTER DON'T
LEAVE

UNTIL MORNING

THE FLOOR THE BED AND ALL ELSE IN BETWEEN
YOU KISS ME THERE AND I HOLD BACK SCREAMS
FEEL SO

GOOD IT HAS TO BE A DREAM
YOU HAVE HER ALWAYS AND I FOR JUST THIS

NIGHT

MAYBE TWO WRONGS WILL NEVER BE RIGHT

UNTIL MORNING

I JUST WANT TO FEEL IT, TOUCH IT, SEE IT, TASTE IT, I PROMISE NOT TO WASTE IT

ALL OF ME

INTELLIGENCE IS ATTRACTIVE
HIS INTELLECT IS STIMULATING
HIS CHOICE OF WORDS CAN EASILY BE
CONSIDERED POETRY AT ITS BEST
TO A CAPTIVATED AUDIENCE HE SPEAKS
I WATCH AND ADORE HIM
HEART R ACING LEGS SHAKING LIPS PUCKER
I WANT TO SUCK THE LIFE OUT OF HIM AND LOVE
HIM BACK TO LIFE
HE NEEDS ME FOR NOW AND I, HIM
THOSE WHO USE WORDS TO SEDUCE HIM MUST
SIT, SHAKE AND WAIT

TALK TO ME

HE SPEAKS TO ME AND MY HEART LISTENS
THE STROKE OF THE KEYS AS HE PUTS HIS
FEELING TO VISUALIZE MAKES MY INNER QUIVER
I MEET HIM IN MY DREAMS WHERE
WE SLOW DANCE INTO PASSION
NEEDING TO HAVE HIM ANY WAY POSSIBLE
HIS LIPS HIS CHEST HIS TOES
EACH AND EVERY HAIR ON HIS BODY WILL
BELONG TO ME SOON ENOUGH
I AM TOTALLY AND COMPLETELY INTO HIS BEING
DO WITH ME WHAT YOU WILL AND I WILL
FOLLOW
MY MOUNTAINS CRUMBLE AND MY OCEAN BEGS
TO BE EXPLORED BY HIM

A DELICIOUS NIGHT

CANDLE LIGHT

SIPS WINE

SEX DEFINED

TAKE TIME

SPREAD MINE

LOVE LIKE THIS

LUST LIKE THIS

WE LIKE THIS

BE LIKE THIS

RIGHT TIME

YOU'RE PRIME

GET BEHIND

SLOW GRIND

NOW DOUBLE TIME

LETS REDEFINE

YOURS AND MINE

Let's Go

Fire in the way he handles a verse Sex
appeal that can't be rehearsed Slapping the
ass of every metaphor
Spitting sexy lyrics as he walks through
the door
Caught my eye the very first time Knew
destiny would make him mine Even if only
one time
Letting him play with my hearts strings
Then night could only bring one thing One
time was all it took
Had him ready for a second and third look
Maybe he thought I was a rook
Blue pill red pill doesn't really matter
Drove him crazy call me the Madd Hatter
Bringing him to his knees is what I desire
He twisted trying to put out this fire
Thought he was a man?
Sucking on his thumb like a little boy
Fuck Joan of who? I'm Helen of Troy!

WINE TIME

SIPS OF YOU ARE AS SWEET AS THE WINE ON MY LIPS

I GET INTOXICATED WHILE LISTENING TO PASSION AND PAIN COMBINED

YOUR SWEAT SENDS MY SOUL SEARCHING FOR MORE

YOU NEVER LEAVING ME WANTING

HAPPILY REFILL YOUR CUP WITH ALL OF ME

I TILT MY GLASS IN HOPES OF SECURING THE LAST DROP OF YOU

UNTIL YOUR REACH OVER AND POUR UNTIL I CAN'T TAKE ANYMORE

SWEETNESS

COME HERE SWEETNESS
ALLOW ME TO EXPRESS ME TO YOU
I AM WHAT YOU THOUGHT YOU COULD WALK
AWAY FROM
I WILL BE STANDING IN THE FORM OF POETRY
WHEN THE DUST SETTLES
I WANT TO WRAP THICK POEMS AROUND YOUR
WAIST AND ALLOW YOU TO FEEL THE WETNESS OF
VERSES SLOWLY BEGINNING TO FORM FROM THE
DARKNESS

DUE TO THE LAST LINES YOU SPIT
YOU HAVE ME
YOU HAD ME
YOU NEED ME BUT YOU DON'T WANT ME
YOU FEEL ME KISSING YOUR NECK SOFTLY AS THE
SPRING WIND YOU FEEL ME BLOWING AS
SMOOTHLY AS AN AUTUMN WIND DAMN BABY

LET NIMA MOAN TO YOU THE STYLE OF POETRY
THAT MAKES YOU FEEL LIKE WE ARE IN A DARK
ROOM WITH THAT GREEN LIGHT LIT AND ONLY
OUR VOICES EMBRACE IN THAT SEXY FUCK FLOW
THAT YOU AND ONLY YOU CAN BRING OUT OF ME

MAKE LOVE TO ME
MY BODY AND SOUL YOU TAKE
REMINDING ME OF HOW GOOD IT USE TO BE
AND HOW OUR DANCE HAS NOT CHANGED
IT IS THE WELCOMING REMINDER OF HOME
YOUR VOICE MAKES ME WANT TO (JILL SCOTT
YOU INTO CHORUS) FEELING LIKE (BILLIE HOLIDAY
AS I LOOK INTO THEM THERE EYES)

Eventually poetry will set this soul on fire and poetry will be the only thing to put out the flame

THE S FACTOR

SLOWLY
SLIPPING
SEDUCTIVELY
SURRENDERING
SENSUOUSLY
SURROUNDED
SUPER NOVA
SUPREMACY SEEKING
SLEEPLESS SUNSETS
SATURATED SEX
SMOOTH SILL
SATIN SHEETS
SECRET SIGHTINGS
SUBLIMINAL SAYINGS
SONGS SUNG SWEETLY
SEEPING INTO SENSES
WE BE BLISS

COMPLETELY AND FOREVER IN A DAY IN LOVE

*I WALKED INTO HIS EYES LONGING AND
WONDERING BUT TRYING TO GET MY SEDUCTIVE
GROWN WOMAN ON*

HE SAW RIGHT THROUGH ME

*IS IT BECAUSE I WANTED TO BE TRANSPARENT OR
WAS HE REALLY THAT VERSED IN ME?*

*SWEAT SLOWLY DANCED DOWN MY FACE, I
HOPING HE WONT NOTICE*

*ONE TOUCH ONE KISS ONE HUG WITH ME PRESSED
AGAINST HIS CHEST
HOLDING ME TIGHT
I FEEL SO SECURE
I LEFT MY LIFE PRESERVER ASHORE*

*ALONG WITH MY LIFE JACKET KNOWING I CAN'T
SWIM
MY EYES I WANTED HIM TO SEE
MY HEART FELT WHAT IT WANTED TO FEEL
I SAW SIGNS OF FOREVER AND NOT FOR THE TIME
BEING*

*WAS MY CHICKEN LESS JUICY BECAUSE I DIDN'T
PRE- HEAT MY OVEN?*

*WAS MY HABITAT NOT SPACIOUS ENOUGH FOR
TIME AWAY BUT NOT REALLY AWAY?*

MY ARMS COULDN'T HOLD HIM TIGHT ENOUGH

MY KISSES DIDN'T CONSUME HIM BUT HE DID ALL THAT FOR ME, BECAUSE HE COULD AND I LET HIM

I WAS COMPLETELY AND FOREVER IN A DAY IN LOVE

HE WALKED AWAY AND I AM COMPLETELY AND FOREVER IN A DAY IN LOVE

YES BABY

HE LOVES PLAYING HIDE AND SEEK WITH HIS PEN
I LOVE TO FIND IT KNOWING THAT HE IS ABOUT
TO WRITE A MASTERPIECE
JUST THE TIP EXCITES MY NERVOUS SYSTEM
HE SLOWLY INSERTS THE TIP INTO INK AND WE
FLOW EFFORTLESSLY
HE WRITES MOUNTAINS AND MY STREAMS RAN
DEEP
YES BABY!
WRITE THAT SHIT OUT ALL NIGHT BABY

UNTITLED

I HAVE SOMEHOW TASTED VISIONS ON HIS LIPS
FIRM HANDS THAT GRASP MY HIPS
PULLED ME CLOSE
DAMN!
I WANT TO DOUBLE DOSE
ENERGY FELT THROUGH MY SKIN SSSSSHHHHIT
I WANT ALL OF IT
GOOSEBUMPS LIKE NEVER BEFORE
I KNOW WHAT'S IN STORE
NUMBERS CREATING HAVOC..69,88, 67
9 AND A HALF WEEKS MY ASS OPEN
REFRIGERATOR DOORS LET'S GET ON THE FLOOR
BLINDFOLDS AND ALL
JUST PUT OUT THAT CALL
OH-MY-DAMN DADDY
THAT'S STUFF SWEET AS CANDY
I HAVE A MAJOR SWEET TOOTH

SAY THAT THEN

IF YOU WANT ME TO PUT ON A SEXY SMILE
AND CRAWL TOWARDS YOU

THE WATER I RAN FOR YOUR BATH IS TOO HOT

THE DRINK I MADE YOU HIT THE SPOT

MY LIPS JUICY AS PLUMS

YOU WANT IT? COME GET SOME!

MODEL MY SHOES WITH MY FINGER TIPS SO YOU
CAN GET A BETTER LOOK

MAYBE YOU WANT ME TO MAKE THIS THING DO
WHAT IT DO?

SAY THAT THEN

WRITE ME ALL NIGHT

HIS PEN ANXIOUSLY AWAITS TO BE RELEASE ONTO
MY BLANK SHEET

ME GIVING HIM INSPIRATION ON EVERY LEVEL

HIS TIP BEGINS PERFECT STROKES OF VERSES

FLOW PERFECTLY TO A SOUND OF MY APPROVAL

MY MOANS BECOME LOUDER AS HE SHARPENS HIS
SKILLS

CUM WRITE ME RIGHTEOUS

HUNGER

*He makes me feel so sexy We be wet in
love all night Moves like satin
Skin like silk
He likes cream
Devours deserts before the main dish Refill
his plates and he asks for more Giving, I am
indeed to his request
We dine all night until full*

SIPS OF HIM

HE ELEVATES MY MIND FROM TIME TO TIME LIKE
COGNAC
LIKE SIPS OF FINE WINE
INTOXICATED ME DULLS MY SENSES REFUSED TO
LET ME GO IN MY INNER PEACE
HE IS MY PEACE
DOES SHE KNOW THAT I WANT YOU?

OOOOOH

YOU ARE WITH ME AND HAVE BEEN
NO APOLOGIES FOR THAT
I LOVE YOU
MY BODY IS CRAVING YOU AND MY MIND GOES TO
THAT PLACE
MY TOES CURL BY THEMSELVES
MY LOWER LIP BITING IS INCREASED THE BODY
WANTS WHAT IT WANTS BLUE PACK WON'T FIT
GOLD IS YOUR COLOR
MAGNUM SIZE FOR MAGNUM EMOTIONS

ME

My sexuality is a tad bit much for some
I make no apologies for that
Sometimes I talk too much when I should
just lay back

My hands in the air ready for whatever
But what I wanted most was me and him
together

I always thought that I wouldn't go down
without a fight But seeing things made me
buckle at the end of the night

Pain follows me to my dressing room
I hide my face in shame

I guess my trainer should have taught me
better
I fell victim to game

MUSIC

MY MOANS RACE HIS MOANS TO THE SURFACE
WE GRAB THEM WITH OUR TONGUES AND
COMBINE WORDS
MY CHEST BEGINS TO RISE AND FALL AT A RAPID
PACE
MY EXCITEMENT SCARES HIM AND SENDS HIM
INTO A FEVERISH MOTION
WE CLAW AND GRAB AT EMOTIONS STILL LEFT
BEHIND PUSHING AND PULLING AT LUST MAKING
LOVE TO LOVE LOVING WORDS
CREATING NEW WORDS TO LOVE LOVING HIS
WORDS HE LETS WORDS WRAP ME IN HIS
SOUL AND IT IS AS IF I AM WRAPPED IN MUSIC

ME AND MY BOO

Where you at? I need dat!
Can't you hear the puuurr of the kitty cat?
Put your head on my mommy's lap
Let me take the pain away while I rub
your back
Soft kisses up and down your spine

My next move is gonna blow your mind
Even if it's for a short time Naw daddy we
go all night I'm well equipped
I don't bring knives to a gunfight
Sit back relax let me rub your feet

Let me throw a tee shirt over these
panties and fix you a little something to
eat
Now fall back close your eyes
Put your hands on my thighs
Like cake to an oven
Watch that shit rise

SEX

HE PULLED ME IN WITH THAT VORTEX OF SEX
GOT ADDICTED TO BEING WET
STAYED WITH A POCKET OF PROTECTS
DIDN'T GIVE A FUCK IF IT WAS 4 IN THE
MORNING
I WAS DEFINITELY OPENING THE DOOR FOR HIM
HE BE DAT SENSITIVE THUG FROM STOMPING
NIGGAS GOT THEM DIRTY BOOTS
NO SHOW OFF
BUT HE KEEPS THAT LOOT
LONG DICKIN ME DOWN
HE GOES POUND FOR POUND
I'M DONE BY THE 3RD ROUND
UP TO MY EARS I FEEL HIM COMING
HE GRIPS THIS BIG ASS
AND TELLS ME TO STOP RUNNING

FLIP SIDE

SCRATCHES ON YOUR BACK
NEVER MIND THAT
ME NO FINGERNAILS
HANDCUFFS ON THE NIGHT STAND WHAT'S THE
GAME PLAN HANGING OUT WITH THE FELLAS IT'S
A GUY THING
IN YOUR POCKET GOES THE WEDDING RING
YOU JUST CALLED YOUR HOMIE YOU AIN'T SEEN IN
A WHILE
I PICK UP THE PHONE AND CAN'T PRESS REDIAL
FLIP THE SCRIPT
MY TURN TO DIP
NOW I'M PLOTTING BITING MY BOTTOM LIP
I AIN'T GONNA TRIP
BRING NO DRAMA TO THE CRIB
JUST KNOW WHEN MY WALK LOOKS A LITTLE
FUNNY.. I DONE DID WHAT I DID

ALL I WANT

ALL I WANT TO DO IS HAVE
A DRINK OR TWO

DO HIS NAILS AND FEET
FIGHT WITH HIM IN THE SHEETS

WASH HIS HAIR
LET HIM KNOW HOW MUCH I CARE

RUB HIS BACK AND HIS DICK NEXT POSITION HE
CAN PICK KISS HIS LIPS

TALK DIRTY IN HIS EAR
LET HIM SMACK ME ON THE REAR

ALL I WANT TO DO IS GET CLOSE ENOUGH TO
SLOW DANCE
ALL I'M ASKING FOR IS ONE CHANCE

SEE ME

CAN YOU SEE ME?

CAN YOU SEE ME WANTING? SEE ME WRITING

*FOLLOW MY FINGERS AS I TRACE TERRITORY
NEEDED TO BE EXPLORED BY YOU ONLY*

*ALLOW YOUR CREATIVE JUICES TO FLOW AND I
PROMISE TO FOLLOW*

FANTASIES UNFOLD BETWEEN US

LAY YOUR BURDENS DOWN ON THE FLOOR

WE WILL MAKE POETRY ON TOP OF THEM

LOVE IS

LOVE IS BEAUTIFUL
LOVE IS WARM AND KIND
LOVE IS HOLDING HANDS WHILE WALKING IN THE
RAIN
UPS AND DOWNS
I ONLY WANT YOU IN MY BED
DO I LOVE YOU?
AS LONG AS WE ARE IN THIS BED

RELATIONSHIP BS

FUCK THIS RELATIONSHIP SHIT

KNEW FROM THE JUMP WE WERE NOT A GOOD
FIT
SAW THE BULGE IN YOUR PANTS
AND JUST COULDN'T HELP IT
JUDGING STARTS HERE
YOU WERE MY BIGGEST FEAR
IT'S LOVE BECAUSE I LOVE TO FUCKIN HATE YOU
WISH I NEVER DATED YOU
POLITICALLY INCORRECT?
ALL YOU WANTED WAS THE SEX
HANDCUFF SHIT I WANNA BUST YOUR FUCKIN LIP
ALL THIS SHIT FOR SOME OK DICK
JUST BECAUSE I COULDN'T GET A GRIP I'M GLAD
YOU LEFT MY ASS, AIN'T SHIT I JUST PULL THE
TOYS OUT MY STASH RELATIONSHIPS FOR THE
BIRDS
NO MORE POETRY
NO MORE WORDS

SO SERIOUS

MY LIPS DO DRIP WITH EXCITEMENT WHILE
INVITING MY MAN GAZING UPON THEM HE
BEGINS TO DIP STICKS IN CHOCOLATE ACTING
REAL CRAZY AND TREATING ME SHADY
BECAUSE I GOT IT BAD FOR THAT ASS
I WANT HIM 8 DAYS
366 DAYS A YEAR
25 HOURS A DAY
MY WISH IS TO PUT HIM IN MY BAG AND PULL
HIM OUT WHEN NEEDED

FIVE STEPS

FIVE STEPS AWAY FROM ECSTASY
SWEAT DRIPS FROM MY BROW IN ANTICIPATION OF
THE NEXT HOURS
THE NEXT HOURS BELONG TO US
INTIMIDATION AND EXCITEMENT FILLS MY NOSTRILS
YOUR AROMA AROUSE MY SENSES
HANDS GRASPING
SHEETS CLINGING TO WET BODIES FROM LOVES
IMPOSSIBLE
LOVE AND LUST IS OUR SOUNDTRACK WELCOMING
DAYBREAK AFTER DAYBREAK TASTING AWAKENING
LIPS
HALF OPENED BLINDS
I RUSH TO CLOSE THEM HOPING TO CAPTURE LAST
NIGHTS EVENTS
CRACKING THE WINDOW JUST A BIT TO CLEAR
THE AIR OF SEX, OIL, AND LEFT OVER TAKE-OUT
SWEETER THAN THE SMELL OF FRESH CUT
FLOWERS

MOSCATO

YOU ARE MY MOSCATO
SWEET TO MY TASTE BUDS

YOU ARE ON MY LIPS
IN MY DEEPEST OF THOUGHTS
DRUNKEN OFF OF YOUR WORDS AND INTOXICATED
BY YOUR GESTURE
I DANCE A SLOW RHYTHM IN MY BED ON MY
SOLO WISHING YOU WERE THERE
TOUCHING MYSELF IN HONOR OF YOU
MY LIPS PART AND SPEAK YOUR NAME OFTEN
LIPS WET WITH ANTICIPATION

MOSCATO

YOU MAKE MY HEAD DELICIOUSLY SWIRL
THE SMELL OF YOU IN THE AIR
THOUGH IT IS ONLY THROUGH MY IMAGINATION
MAKES ME HIGH

MY NEEDS

TODAY I AWAKE WITH URGES THAT HAVE
INVADED MY DREAMS ALL THROUGH THE NIGHTS
I HAVE TAKEN HIS WORDS AND WENT TO BED
WITH THEM
HE HAS PURPOSELY LEFT ME WANTING AND
NEEDING A RELEASE
HE MUST BE MY RELEASE VISIONS OF PROMISES
MADE WORDS EXCHANGED
NEED HIS PICTURE TO FIT THIS FRAME
URGES SURGING
MY FINGERTIPS WANT TO PRESS AGAINST HIS LIPS
AS I TRACE THEM TO HIS TRUE FEELINGS
WONDERING HAS NEVER BEEN MY THING
I WONDER STILL
MY WANTS AND NEEDS ARE AT A SIZZLE
I WAIT

NOUNS AND VERBS

HIS WORDS DID EXCITE ME
HOW I FANTASIZED OF MAKING LOVE TO HIS
WORDS IN MY EAR
LAYING MY BODY ON A BED OF SEXY ADJECTIVES
PULLING ME CLOSER AS HE CONTINUOUSLY THRUST
VERBS INTO MY INNERMOST
I BECOMING HIS HOST FOR NOUNS
SPOKEN WORD AWAITS ME IN THE SOFT OF A
PILLOW
POETRY SPRINKLED ACROSS THE CARPET SLOW
EROTIC MOVEMENT STIMULATES
HIS DISTINCTIVE PLEASURE SOURCE AWAKENS MY
SOUL AND IGNITE THE FIRE DEEP WITHIN
ATTEMPTS TO WALK AWAY SEEM UNNATURALLY
UNREALISTIC
WANTING TURNING INTO NEEDING
NEEDING TURNING ON ME
HIS PRESENCE IS POWERFUL IN MY SLUMBER
HARD TO AWAKE
SO I KEEP DREAMING
THIS IS OUR ONLY TIME TOGETHER
HE IS SO CLOSE YET SO FAR AWAY
I ADORE HIM AND HE DOES NOT KNOW OR COULD
CARE LESS

UNIVERSAL

Our suns burn for one another
Our moons glow because of the others
illumination
My eyes twinkle
He crashes thunderous waves through me
When we are done my calming seas puts him
to sleep...
Damn I am still horny

NEEDS

*TAKING A STEP BACK AND STEPPING OUTSIDE OF
ME HAS BOUGHT A PICTURE INTO FOCUS
MY WANTS TURNED INTO NEEDS AND LEFT ME
NEEDING WHAT I WANTED
TRYING TO FILL UP AN ENDLESS CUP WITH MY
POTION COULD NEVER REALLY WORK
I BEING STUBBORN AND FREE SPIRITED ATTEMPTED
REGARDLESS
IMAGES AND VISIONS DANCED IN MY HEAD AS A
WHITE MAN WITH A RED SUIT AND BAG FULL OF
TOYS TO CHILDREN THAT BELIEVED
I SOMETIMES SAT AS THE SPOOK BEHIND THE
DOOR GATHERING INFORMATION HOPING IT
WOULD GIVE ME SOME SORT OF LEVERAGE
UNFORTUNATELY NONE OF MY FINDINGS HAVE
SERVED ME IN ANY WAY
I AM SADDENED BY THIS
LIFE HAPPENS*

DUDE

HE IS THAT DUDE
HIS SHIT REAL SMOOTH
WALKS IN THE ROOM
GETS YOUR WOMAN'S ATTENTION
DID I MENTION? THE WAY HE LOOKS MY PANTIES
SHOOK
WANTED TO TAKE THEM OFF RIGHT THEN AND
THERE
HE WHISPERED IN MY EAR
I HAVE A SECRET TO SHARE
FELT LIKE I WAS FLOATING TO THE DOOR WHO
KNEW WHAT HE HAD IN STORE SILENCE WAS MY
CLAIM TO FAME UNTIL HE BEAT THIS OUT THE
FRAME
WORKED WONDERS WITH THE DICK
HAD NO PROBLEM BEING THE 2ND 3RD OR 4TH
CHICK
I SWEAR FOR A SECOND THOUGHT ABOUT TAKING
OFF THE CONDOM AND HAVING SOME SEEDS
THEN REALIZED IT JUST WASN'T ME
AND THIS TYPE OF DUDE HAS TO BE FREE
HIT IT ALL TYPES OF CRAZY
MUSIC WE MADE
COLORS WE BLENDED
I WAS FUCKED UP WHEN IT ALL ENDED
HAD ME PANTING HIS NAME
STOPPED RIGHT AT THE TIP AND ASKED
ME..(WHAT'S MY NAME?) I LOOKED AT HIM AS HE
LOOKED AT ME
ALL OUT OF BREATH I WHISPERED...

"POETRY"

JUST WORDS

LIE TO ME WHEN WE MAKE LOVE
TELL ME YOU LOVE ME
TELL ME I BELONG TO YOU AND YOU BELONG TO
ME
TELL ME THAT YOU ARE MY FOREVER
WITH YOUR LIPS SAY THAT UNLESS GOD CALLS
YOU HOME OR THE DEVIL BECKONS TO YOU THAT
NOTHING WILL COME BETWEEN US
TELL ME NOW AND I PROMISE TO BELIEVE YOU
I PROMISE TO FUCK HARDER BUT I NEED A LITTLE
INCENTIVE TO INITIATE

YOUR MAN

CRISS–CROSS APPLESAUCE
CAN YOUR MAN COME OUT AND PLAY
I KNEW HE WAS YOUR MAN WHEN I SPOTTED
Y'ALL THE OTHER DAY
HE JUST SO DAMN FINE
I JUST WANT A LITTLE OF HIS TIME
I DON'T NEED TO MAKE HIM, MINE
LISTEN TO HIM TALK
THAT BODY
THE, WAY HE STANDS, DAMN!
WHAT'S THAT SCENT HE WEARS? I DON'T CARE
I JUST WANT TO CALL HIM AND LISTEN TO HIM
BREATH ON THE PHONE
I CAN PRETEND THAT WE ARE ALONE
GIRL YOU BETTER KEEP HIM IN THE HOUSE
BECAUSE THIS CAT WILL BE ALL OVER THAT
MOUSE (MEOW)

THIS FEELING

THIS FEELING CRIPPLING ME
HIS NON EXISTENT PHYSICAL FORM
THIS LONELY ESCAPADE IN A DIM LIT ROOM
TALKING TO THE WALLS PRETENDING HE CAN
HEAR ME
TOUCHING MY SELF UNTIL MY FINGERS DISAPPEAR
WISHING THEY WERE HIS
HOLDING MY PILLOW BETWEEN MY LEGS
THIS FEELING STAYS WITH ME
HE COULD NEVER KNOW
I WISH HE COULD
NEED HIM HARD AND STEADY
I'M SO READY
LIPS MEET UNTIL HE LIFTS HIS HEAD TO SAY...
CUM FOR ME
I WILL DEFINITELY CUM FOR HIM

HAVE WE MET?

*I WANT TO HOLD YOU UNTIL WE ARE NO LONGER
TWO
KISS YOU AS IF MY LIFE DEPENDS UPON IT
GAZE INTO YOUR EYES AS IF THEY HOLD THE
SECRETS OF LIFE
I NEED TO BURY MY NOSE INTO YOUR SKIN UNTIL
YOU HAVE NO SCENT LEFT AND ALL THAT YOU
HAD NOW LIVES WITHIN ME
CAPTURING YOUR VOICE IN AJAR JUST OPENING IT
TO HEAR YOU SAY*

I LOVE YOU

*FEELING YOU PULLING ME CLOSER SO THAT WE
ARE FACE TO FACE AND I CAN SMELL THE DESIRE
COMING FROM YOUR BREATH
I CAN FEEL THE WANT BENEATH YOUR WAIST
NOTICING MY HEAVY BREATHING, YOU ATTEMPT TO
SOOTH AND CALM
ITS NOT WORKING
YOU ARE ALL TOO FAMILIAR TO MY SPIRIT
I JUST CAN'T SHAKE IT
IT'S COMFORTING AND INVITING
ITS BLUE SKIES AND WHITE CLOUDS
ITS RAINDROPS ON A LAZY SUNDAY MORNING
QUESTION...*

HAVE WE MET?

Chapter 2

YESTERDAY AND TODAY

MOTHERS AND FATHERS CRY
BABIES DIE BOTTLES FLY PRAYERS TO SKIES WE
ALL WE GOT
COPS RING OUT SHOTS
YOUNG GUNS GO POP

HANDS IN THE AIR DON'T YOU DARE... MAKE A
MOVE NIGGER HANDS ON MY TRIGGER

ONE BLAST WILL PUT YOU ON THE GROUND
YOU WON'T HEAR A SOUND
THOSE TEARS DON'T MEAN SHIT TO ME
THE BOTTOM OF MY BOOT IS WHERE YOUR HEAD
SHOULD BE
IF I HAD MY WAY YOU WOULD SWING FROM A
TREE

TAR BABY
DADDY'S MAYBE
WE TAUGHT YOU TO HATE YOUR OWN KIND
THAT'S WHY YOU CRAZY

YOU PEOPLE ALWAYS WANT TO PROTEST
WHILE WE STAND BEHIND WITH OUR GUNS UP
YOUR MAMMA DRESS
I DID IT TO YOUR GRANDMOTHER AND HER
MOTHER BEFORE THAT GO ON AND MAKE A FUSS
ALL YOU IS...

IS BLACK

I WISH

*I WISH I COULD SAY...THANK YOU FOR FIGHTING
FOR ME
I WISH I COULD TELL THOSE THAT USE THIS
SITUATION FOR THEIR OWN SELFISH PURPOSES TO
STOP! I WISH I COULD TAKE AWAY THE HURT
AND ANGER THAT YOU ALL FEEL INSIDE
I WISH I COULD START MY FIRST DAY OF COLLEGE
AND CHECK OUT THE FEMALES STEPPING HARD
I WISH I WOULD HAVE WRITTEN THAT POEM
THAT MY BOYS CLOWNED ME ABOUT
I WISH I COULD WIPE THE TEARS FROM MY
MOTHER'S EYES
I WISH HER SON DIDN'T HAVE TO DIE
WHY???
WE PAY YOU TO PROTECT AND SERVE
TO KEEP ORDER
YOU SERVED ME BULLETS OVER AND OVER
SOMEONE ELSE WILL SIT IN MY SEAT ON THE
FIRST DAY OF CLASS*

PASS THE L'S

LOYALTY AND LOVE
PONDER THE DEFINITION OF THE TWO AND
CHOOSE BETWEEN

HE SAID HE LOVED HER BUT THAT WAS THE
FURTHEST THING FROM HIS MIND

SAID YOUR SWEET SO ROUGH DRIVES ME IN SANE
BUT IT WAS ALL A GAME

REMINDED HER OF HER UP BRINGING· AND SHE
WALKED AROUND IN A HAZE

YOU REMIND ME OF MY MOM
WOULD YOU TREAT YOUR MOTHER THIS WAY?
THOUGHT HE HAD EVERYTHING IN PLACE
BUT YOU CAN'T HOLD THE MOON AND STARS

WHY SHOULD YOU BE ALLOWED TO HOLD ME?
IN THE END TOO MANY HAVE BEEN ON THE LIST
OF TO DO

OUR LOVE AND APPRECIATION FOR WORDS PUT
US IN THE LINE OF FIRE AND SOMETIMES WE
FORGET TO DUCK

STALKER TYPE

I WATCHED HIS PAGE AND THE COMMENTS MADE
DON'T LIKE WHAT I SEE
I DEFINITELY THROW SHADE RANT AND RAVE
UNTIL HE CAVE THEN I'M DOING THE SAME SHIT
SAME TYPE MOVES MADE
JUST LIKE HIM
JUST LIKE ME
DON'T CARE HOW IT'S SUPPOSE TO BE
I DO WHAT I DO BECAUSE I'M A SEASONED VET
SIS THINKS SHE IS WEARING THE CROWN
CAN'T BECAUSE I AIN'T GIVE IT UP YET
I GIVE YOU THIS MUCH
YOU'RE ON HIS MIND
BUT ONCE I GET MY HANDS ON HIM THAT ASS IS
MINE
I AIN'T GIVING SHIT UP TIL I'M DONE
WHO TOLD YOU TO PULL A KNIFE WHEN I'M
HOLDING A GUN?
YOU HOLDING DIAMONDS WHILE I'M HOLDING
SPADES
YOU SUSPECT ON THE STRIP AND YOU JUST GOT
MADE
IN OTHER WORDS..
FALL BACK AND RELAX AND TAKE A SEAT
YOU STILL GOT HIM UNTIL HE AND I MEET
I LOVE BEEF

HIM

I LOVE HIM AND IT'S DEEP
I AM SO LOST WITHOUT HIM BUT I WILL NEVER
TELL HIM THAT STANDING GROUND ITS VITAL
BEING STRONG IS MY FOCUS HE INVADES MY
DREAMS HE HOLDS ME HOSTAGE
HE IS THE KEEPER OF MY SMILE
SUNNY DAYS ARE A LITTLE LESS BRIGHT
I MISS MY SPARKLE

YOU DID THIS

YOUR WORDS JUMPED OFF OF MY SCREEN AND
TOUCHED MY INNER THOUGHTS
VOICE SO MELLOW AND CREAM FILLED
YOUR TOUCH IS ELECTRICALLY CONNECTED TO MY
MAIN FRAME
PUSHING ALL THE RIGHT BUTTONS AND WATCHING
ME WORK
SEEING YOU AND CONNECTING THE DOTS MAKES
ME WANT TO COUNT TO 100
BUT I HAVE TO TAKE YOUR CLOTHES OFF NOW

PLAYING GAMES

WE TWO COULD PLAY WITH HAPPINESS
YOU COULD HOLD ME A PORTION OF FOREVER
LATE NIGHT POETRY
EARLY MORNING FANTASIES COFFEE IN YOUR CUP
CREAM WITHIN ME
HE COULD HAVE ME TOTALLY ON HIM
UNDER HIM
SIDE BY SIDE
COULD YOU ALLOW ME TO GIVE YOU A BATH?
WASH YOUR BACK
RUB YOU WHEN IT HURTS TELL ME WHAT WORKS
KISS YOU THERE
I DON'T CARE
RUB AND SOOTH
YOU BEEN IN THE MOOD
I GUARANTEE YOU WILL CALL HER BY MY NAME
NO TWO WOMEN ARE THE SAME
I KNEW THE RULES OF THE GAME
I'M PLAYING JUST THE SAME UNTIL YOU RIP THIS
SHIT OUT THE FRAME

CRAZY FOR HIM

HE DO GOT A SISTER ACTING ALL TYPE OF
IRRATIONAL
SUBLIMINALLY SPEAKING IN HUSH TONES
PLACING UNWANTED TITLES OVER HIM BECAUSE I
NEED FOR HIM TO SEE THINGS MY WAY
ATTEMPTING TO ENCOURAGE SECRET SESSIONS
SEXUAL FANTASIES CONTROLLING MY EMOTIONAL
STATUS
HE TOO BUSY TO ACKNOWLEDGE MY INNER
THOUGHTS AND TOO BUSY EXPRESSING AND
SHARING THOUGHT ON THE OTHER SIDE
I WAIT PATIENTLY ASSUMING HE CARES
MY IGNORANCE ALLOWS ME TO CONTINUE TO
WAIT FOR A LETTER AS IF HE IS AWAY AT THE
WAR
YELLING FOR THE COACH TO PUT ME IN THE
GAME STANDING ON DISPLAY TO SHOW HIM MY
WARES WHEN WILL HE SHOW ME HIS WARES?

THE I LOVE YOU BLUES

BLOOD FAMILY LOVE PET OWNER /PET LOVE
APPRECIATION LOVE POETIC LOVE
I HAVE A BLUES IN MY BEING FOR HIS LOVE
NOT THAT PEACE AND BLESSINGS LOVE
BUT THAT BABY IT IS YOU WHO I CHOOSE AND
PRAY YOU CHOOSE ME
AND WE CHOOSE WE LOVE
THAT LETS WALK IN THE RAIN LET ME PRICK MY
FINGERS ON A THORN BECAUSE YOU DESERVE
THOSE FLOWERS LOVE
LET'S TAKE A SHOWER WITH OUR CLOTHES ON
TOGETHER LOVE
KISSING PASSIONATELY AS IF MY KISSES WILL
SAVE HIS LIFE
THE PROBLEM WITH THAT DEEP ROOTED
SUBMERGED TYPE LOVE IS THAT IT; HURTS MORE
WHEN YOU FALL APART
BUT LOVE –REAL LOVE TAKES CHANCES, GRABS
LIFE AND STARES IT IN THE EYES AND SAYS...
HERE I STAND!
I AM NOT AFRAID
WIN LOSE DRAW I'M FINE WITH IT BECAUSE I
LOVE AND THERE IS NOTHING YOU CAN DO ABOUT
IT
WRITE ME OLD FASHION LOVE NOTES AND READ
THEM TO ME WHEN WE SPEAK
NO REHEARSAL
STUMBLE OVER YOUR WORDS BECAUSE YOU ARE
NERVOUS AND THIS IS A FIRST. LOVE
LET MY WATERS QUENCH YOUR THIRST
LET ME FEED YOU CHICKEN SOUP WHEN YOU ARE
SICK
KISS YOU DOWN TO YOUR....

HOOD NOVEL

IMAGINATION
IN HER PRIME SHE SITS AND WAITS
ANTICIPATION DRIPS SLOWLY
HOPING ONLY HE WILL CATCH HER SCENT IN THE
AIR
SHE FINDS HER IMAGINATION TAKING CONTROL
CAUSING HER TO LOSE CONTROL

ATTEMPTS TO REGAIN COMPOSURE FAILS AS SHE
FALLS DEEP INTO HIS VOICE OBEYING HIS EVERY
COMMAND IN HOPES THAT HER REWARDS SHALL
COME SWIFTLY IN HIS BEDROOM

SHE CARES NOT TO BE PROPER BUT TO BE
COMPLETELY AND TOTALLY ENGULFED WITHIN HIM
JUST HER IMAGINATION KICKING INTO HIGH GEAR
SINCE HE IS NEVER NEAR

SHE HAD BEEN IN

SHE HAD
SAW FROM A FAR AND UP CLOSE TASTED AND
SMELLED ITS AROMA FELT ITS TOUCH
KISSED ITS LIPS OVER AND OVER
FELT ITS EMBRACE
SLOWLY ALLOWING HER SOUL TO DANCE
SPIRIT TO FLY
MELODIES PLAY

THEY TWO SIT AND LISTEN AS SMALL PETALS OF
POSSIBILITIES PASS THROUGH THEIR PALMS
SHARING IDEAS IN NEVER NEVER LAND
BECAUSE THE REALITY OF THEM MAY ONLY EXIST
THERE
SCARS ON HER EMOTIONS

SHE HAS AND WILL GATHER ALL THAT LOVE IS
AND WILL BE AND SHARE IT WITH HIM
AT TIMES SEES HIM SIDEWAYS BECAUSE OF HIS
ACTION
NEEDING TO LISTEN TO HIS HEART BEAT
WANTING TO GAZE INTO HIS EYES
HE NEEDS TO KNOW HOW SHE ADORED HIS BEING

Love My City

Elevated trains through bright and
darkened skies
Subs that run below hiding the truth at
times and running
Through my mental
After visions during the day
My city fans, we go hard or go home
When we love you we love you and when
we hate you ... Our crime rate has
surpassed all of you small time bitches
Catch transportation from, one side of
town to the next They come from all
walks of life to stare at our fish bowl

REAL MEN...DAMN!

SHORT TALL BIG SMALL THUG REFORMED
SENSITIVE AND SWAGGED OUT
PHILLY CHEESE STEAKS, WATER ICE, PRETZELS
AND YOU BOO
TURN MY DARK SKIES BLUE KEEP DOING WHAT
YOU DO ALWAYS ME AND YOU
GO BACK LIKE CHARLESTON CHEW
LIKE SHAGGY AND SCOOBY DO
WE ROCK OUT LIKE FLINT-STONES
YABBA DABBA DOO

CORNER BOY

HE STANDS ON THE CORNER TRYING TO KEEP HIS
FINGERTIPS WARM WITH THE FIRE FROM HIS
NEWPORT
IT'S DARK AND COLD, NOT EVEN A WET HEAD IN
SIGHT.

HE HAS NEVER BEEN A BITCH ASS NIGGA BUT
SOMETHING ABOUT TONIGHT WASN'T RIGHT. HE
HAS BEEN FOR SOMETIME NOW THE TERROR TO
MANY IN THE HOOD BUT TONIGHT HE WAS NOT
THE ONLY BULLY IN THE SCHOOLYARD..

CONVERSATIONS

HE SAID –BABY I LOVE YOU

SHE SAID–I DON'T THINK YOU DO

HE SAID–YOU ARE MY EVERYTHING

SHE SAID–THAT BULLSHIT DON'T MEAN A THING

HE SAID–WHAT ABOUT THE PROMISE TO FORGIVE?

SHE SAID–THAT WAS BEFORE YOU DID WHAT YOU DID

HE SAID–DON'T THROW AWAY ALL THAT WE HAVE BEEN THROUGH

SHE SAID–FUNNY HOW YOU DIDN'T THINK OF THAT WHEN YOU WERE LAYING UP WITH YOUR OTHER BOO OH, YOU DIDN'T THINK THAT I KNEW?

WING WOMAN

WING WOMAN
EXCUSE ME MY FRIEND AND I HAVE BEEN
WATCHING YOU FROM ACROSS THE ROOM
SHE WANTED ME TO TELL YOU THAT YOUR SKIN
LOOKS AS IF IT HAS BEEN KISSED BY THE GODS
YOUR CONFIDENT WALK SCREAMS OF PRIDE
THOSE BEDROOM EYES INVITE HER TO MORE THAN
JUST A DRINK
SHE SAYS SHE CAN SEE HERSELF LYING ACROSS
THE BED WHILE YOU PROP YOUR NOTEBOOK OF
POETRY UPON HER ASS
SHE WILL PRETEND TO WATCH A MOVIE
YOU WILL PRETEND TO WRITE
THE TWO OF YOU WILL FALL IN LOVE
HE LOOKS AND ASKS...
(WHY ARE YOU TALKING IN THE 3RD PERSON?)

NUTS TO SOUP

TOOK A WALK ON THE WILD SIDE
DIDN'T MEAN TO SLIP OR SLIDE |
GOT STUCK ON STUPID
TO EMBARRASSED TO ASK FOR HELP
EMOTIONAL OUTBURST FINGERS POINTED WHO TO
BLAME?
NO SHAME TO EITHER GAME
WANTED EXACTLY WHAT WE RECEIVED
DIDN'T REALIZE MORE WAS WANTED
PLOTTING ON MY DEMISE AS I SEE YOURS JUST
OVER THE HILL
POINTS OF PLEASURE INVESTED
GUMBO WE CALL RELATIONSHIP
WE HUNGER AND TASTE
YOU LOVING EVERY SPOONFUL

I NEVER LIKED GUMBO

3AM..

I BY MY PHONE AND YOU BY YOUR COMPUTER

WE DO A DANCE EXCHANGE AND RUN TO OUR OWN CORNERS OF THE WORLD LOVE HIDE AND SEEK
LOVE BEING DISCOVERED EVEN MORE

YOU ARE THAT ENCHANTED FOREST THAT I RUN THROUGH BAREFOOT AND FREE AS THE WIND

IF BY CHANCE WE STUMBLE AND FALL IN MY CAREFREE
REACH OUT YOUR HAND TO PULL ME CLOSE AND WHISPER "IT'S ABOUT TIME WE MET" BEFORE LETTING ME GO ONCE MORE

MAYBE WE TWO LAY IN GREEN GRASS UNINTERRUPTED BY MAN OR NATURE

LETTING NATURE TAKE ITS COURSE

IT'S 3AM AND YOU RUN THROUGH MY MIND

SALUTE TO THE 80'S

RED TAPE BLUE TAPE HAD IT ON LOCK TURNED
OUT ZOMBIES FROM THAT ROCK SITTING ON THE
STEPS EATING WATER ICE DUDES IN THE ALLEY
SHOOTING DICE
SUMMERS AT GRANDMA'S GAVE ME SO MUCH JOY
SWIMMING POOLS IN SOUTHWEST HAD ALL THE
CUTE BOYS LAZY SUMMERS WITH NOTHING TO DO
THE NIKE BOYS IN BARTRAM VILLAGE HAD THE
FINEST CREW
DARK SKIN BROTHERS WERE MY CHOICE SINCE I
HEARD BIG DADDY KANE'S VOICE LADIES LOVE
COOL JAMES WAS HIS NAME ROCK THE BELLS
DROVE ME IN SANE
DJ JAZZY JEFF & FRESH PRINCE, 3XDOPE, TOUGH
CREW HAD IT HOPPIN! THE AFTER MIDNIGHT
HAD IT POPPIN
SIXERS TOOK THE CHAMPIONSHIP
MCFADDEN & WHITEHEAD–AIN'T NO STOPPING!
WOP IT OUT ALL DAY LONG
AT NIGHT SMOKE IT OUT WATCHING (CHEECH AND
CHONG) POP LOCKING WAS THE DANCE CRAZE
AT HOME MOMS ROCKING (FRANKIE BEVERLY AND
MAZE)
GAVE BIRTH TO MY FIRST BEAUTIFUL BABY GIRL
SHE BECAME MY WHOLE WORLD
IN THE 80'S I FELL IN LOVE WITH TEENA MARIE
LATER KEITH SWEAT HAD ME DOING MY THING
THOUGH HE'S ALWAYS BEEN THE KING
IN THE 80'S MICHAEL JACKSON WAS SUPREME
LOVED THE 80'S AS YOU CAN TRULY SEE
BUT THE 70'S OUT DID THEM BECAUSE IT GAVE
BIRTH TO ME!

MY IMAGINATION

IN MY IMAGINATION WE MAKE LOVE
EACH NIGHT THE MOON BEGINS TO PEEK THROUGH
THE DAYLIGHT; I AWAKE HIM WITH KISSES DOWN
LOW
HE TAKING UP SO MUCH OF MY DAY AND DOESN'T
REALIZE
EXCITED BECAUSE HE HAS PUT A FACE TO WORDS
INVADING YOUR PRIVATE THOUGHTS AND INNER
PEACE
THEY LIE TO YOU AND YOU PRETEND TO BELIEVE
BECAUSE YOU WANT THEM JUST THAT BADLY
HEARING THEM BUT THEY ARE MILES AWAY
TOUCHING THEM YET THEY ARE OUT OF YOUR
REACH
DREAMING OF THEM WHILE THEY ARE DREAMING
OF SOMEONE ELSE
IN MY VISION I SEE DAYS AND NIGHTS THAT WILL
NEVER COME TO PASS

KEEP IT REAL

I'M ON SOME REAL SHIT
NIGGAS KILLS FOR THIS
CAN'T TAKE NO PILLS FOR THIS
SWEET DEEP DISH
CARAMEL ISH
LICK LIPS AFTER THIS
SUCKING FINGERS LOOKING FOR IT
DON'T WANT ANYONE ELSE TO GET NO MORE OF
IT
SOFT, SWEET, AND MOIST
COMING TO YOU
YOU BEGIN TO REJOICE COME TO DADDY DON'T
BE SHY
WE ALL GET A LITTLE CRAZY OVER GRANDMAS
SWEET POTATO PIE
GET Y'ALL MINDS OUT OF THE GUTTER

JUST LIKE THAT

YOU SAW
YOU ADMIRED FOR WHATEVER REASON
PLAYING GAMES IS AN UNFORTUNATE PART OF
LIFE
PAIN AND PLEASURE ALL UP AND THROUGH
NEVER BEEN ONE TO FALL BUT THE SPELL WAS
CAST
AND THIS ASS WAS HAD
MIDDLE FINGER IN THE AIR
FOR ANYONE THAT DIDN'T CARE ABOUT THIS SHIT
WE SHARE
POP REAL FUCKIN FLY WHEN QUESTION WHY?
WHEN YOU ANGRY WITH ME I JUST WANT TO
CRY I HATE THAT HOLD THAT YOU HAVE ON ME
CAN'T SHAKE IT
RIDE THIS SHIT TIL THE WHEELS BUCKLE AND
FALL OFF
THEN BUILD ANOTHER BIKE
PROMISE TO BE BETTER THAN
PROMISE TO DO ALL THE THINGS YOU LIKE
TO YOU JUST ANOTHER CHICK
I HAD THE MAKINGS OF A WIFE! UNSURE OF MY
WORTH THEN
BUT CLEAR ON THAT SHIT NOW!
BURIED MY THOUGHTS OF YOU DEEP IN THE
GROUND
FUCK YOU AND THE DIP YOU RODE IN ON! YOU
AIN'T THAT GUY
YOU NEVER BEEN THAT FLY
BULLSHIT WRAPPED IN SEX APPEAL
YOU TRANSPARENT
I CAN'T STAND IT
I KNOW THE FUCKIN DEAL
YOU AIN'T THAT REAL

Back up before you get fucked up or before you get fucked (lol) I'm so serious

I'M SO SORRY

I am sorry that this comes at a bad time
but.. I like you
I like the way you smell
The way I act as if I have a question to
ask so that you double back and I catch a
hint of your aroma
I like the twinkling in your eye when you
smile
Your words are a safe haven
They are my sanctuary
They use to shelter me
Now they provide shelter for someone else
It's now raining and shelter is what I
seek yet your umbrella walks on the other
side of the street
We find each other for a second in a
glance and though she is surrounded by
your scent and your love..
I still like you

FUNNY THING ABOUT LOVE

YOU LIKE IT

LOVE IT

HATE IT
SIT AND THINK ABOUT IT

TAKE A DRINK BECAUSE OF IT

WISH IT NEVER HAPPENED

JUMP OVER IT TO AVOID IT AND STEP IN A PILE
OF IT

SHIT...CAN'T DO WITHOUT IT

JUST THINK

I THOUGHT FOR A MOMENT THEN TWICE
THE IDEA OF YOU IS SOME WHAT NICE
HOW TO ENCOURAGE THAT SHAFT WITH ALL ITS
ATTACHMENTS TO DWELL IN THESE WATERS FOR A
SPELL OR TWO

TEACH YOU HOW TO DRINK PROPERLY SO THAT
YOU DON'T FORGET YOUR PLACE IN ME TEACH
YOU HOW TO HOLD THESE LIFE GIVING BREASTS
SO THAT YOU REMEMBER TO FLEE FROM ALL
OTHERS

IN ME YOU WILL FIND ALL THAT YOU NEED AND
DESIRE MY LIPS WILL BREATHE NEW LIFE INTO
YOU AND CARRY YOU AWAY FOR A MOMENT. I
PROMISE TO WRAP YOU INTO ME AS WE BECOME
US

ALLOW YOUR BLOOD TO RUSH..FROM YOUR HEAD
BECAUSE THERE IS NO FIGHTING DESTINY
MENTALLY I HAVE YOU YET YOU FIGHT TO STAY
AWAY
ONLY TO HURT YOURSELF IN THE END

YES WHEELS TURNING IDEAS START BURNING
POSSIBLY SOME YEARNING COULD BE THE HOUR
WORDS BEGIN TO SHOWER COULD BE THE HOUR
NEED TO BE PUTTING INTO MOTION

HE STILL TRYING TO FIGURE ME OUT
WANT TO KNOW WHAT BROWN THICKNESS ALL
ABOUT NEVER A HOOD CHICK BUT BE ON SOME
GHETTO SHIT VERY SMART

NEVER UNDER ESTIMATE HER MENTAL SHIT
DON'T LOOK TOO HARD
YOU JUST MAY SLIP
TRIP AND LAND ON HER SPACESHIP

WHEN WE GOING DON'T COST YOU A THING BUT A
MENTAL NOTE
HER SHIT HOOK YOU QUICK SO YOU WANT TO
TAKE A TOTE DAT POETIC SHIT IS KINDA DOPE

I SHED A TEAR

I SHED A TEAR KNOWING SHE'S GOING AWAY
I SHED A TEAR KNOWING SHE REALLY CAN'T STAY
I SHED A TEAR KNOWING THAT WE HAS TOO FEW
CONVERSATIONS
FEELING DEEP INSIDE THAT MY HEART IS
BREAKING
SHED A TEAR BECAUSE ONCE AGAIN MY HEAD IS
ACHING
SHE GREW UP WAY TOO FAST
SPECIAL TIMES THAT WE MISSED
NEVER GOT TO TELL HER WHAT TO EXPECT ON
HER FIRST KISS
NEVER HAD A CHANCE TO TELL HER HOW TO
SPOT LOVE WHEN IT WALKS INTO HER LIFE
TOO LATE TO TELL HER HOW TO MAINTAIN WHO
SHE IS AND STILL BE A GREAT WIFE
I SHED A TEAR BECAUSE SHE IS LEAVING THE
NEST
I THINK OF THE BAD TIMES THAT WE HAVE
OVERCOME YESTER YEARS WHEN SPOKE OF BRINGS
US TO TEARS BRINGING IT BACK TO WHERE IT
ALL BEGAN
MAN SHE HAS SOME PRETTY SKIN AND SOME
WHITE TEETH
PUT THESE YOUNG GIRLS TO SHAME WHEN SHE
WALKS DOWN THE STREET
HER LAUGH IS SO HEARTILY AND TRUE
IF YOU'VE NEVER BEEN IN THE ROOM, WHEN SHE
LAUGHS SHAME ON YOU
I SHED A TEAR BECAUSE I WILL MISS ALL THAT I
SHED A TEAR BECAUSE I WANT HER BACK BUT
FOR NOW I WILL SHED A TEAR

A letter to GOD

You have known me prior to my existence

I still do not know myself

I have looked in the mirror and still can't figure out

Who, where, or what I should be about

I thought I came to your house so many times before

Felt good inside but I still exited unsure

I want to run to you with my arms open wide

If I come to you will you choose to hide?

We have lost contact and I know it's because of me So many times you called and I did not answer

Please do not hole it against me

SCRIPTURE

MY LOVE FOR YOU IS SCRIPTURE YET YOU STILL
DON'T GET THE PICTURE
I WANT TO BUILD PYRAMIDS IN THE NAME OF
YOU
THAT WILL REACH THE HEAVENS AND HAVE THE
ANGELS COMING TO ADMIRE YOU
YET LIKE THE TOWER OF BABEL WE SEEM LOST
AND CONFUSED AS IF OUR LANGUAGES SEPARATED
SOMEWHERE BETWEEN THE FIRST AND THIRD
LEVEL OF US
YOU ASK ME IF I'M HAPPY YET YOU DO NOTHING
TO SUPPORT MY CAUSE
STOP ASKING LIKE YOU REALLY GIVE A DAMN
STOP PERPETRATING A FRAUD PROMISING
FOREVER'S WHEN YOU CAN'T EVEN GIVE ME
TOMORROWS CARING OR WANTING ME WHEN IT'S
CONVENIENT FOR YOU
BEGGING ME TO BREAK ALL THE RULES WHEN
YOU DO NOTHING TO SUPPORT WHAT I DO
FIRE IN MY EYES BECAUSE OF ANGER THAT YOU
HELPED TO FUEL
REALITY SETS IN AND HEARTACHE BEGINS
COLORS OF LOVE ARE LOST AND WHAT'S LEFT
BEGINS TO BLEND
CATCH 22 IS IN CONTINUOUS ROTATION
YET I TRY TO CHANGE THE RADIO STATION ONLY
TO HEAR LOVE AGAIN
I MISS YOU
I NEED YOU
I WANT YOU SUNG BY MY FAVORITE ARTIST
SENDING ME BACK
THE BOOK OF GENESIS SPEAKS OF HOW GOD
CREATED ALL THINGS AND ON THE 7TH DAY HE
RESTED HE CREATED US IN HIS IMAGE. IS THIS

*THE REASON FOR ME TO YELL FOR GOD WHEN
YOU LOVE ME SO DEEP?
MOUNTAIN TOPS OF REGRET YET I WANT YOUR
HANDS, LIPS, KISSES THAT WONT LET ME FORGET
SMELLING YOUR SCENT
MAKING ME WET
TELLING MYSELF NEVER LOOK BACK
LOTS WIFE GOT CAUGHT UP LIKE THAT
LET ME RUN MY FINGERS THROUGH YOUR CURLY
LOCKS
COME PLAY IN THIS BOX
ALL I WANT TO DO IS LAY
LAY MY LOVE ON THE LINE JUST ONE MORE TIME
THEY DON'T UNDERSTAND THAT I ADORE YOU–MI
AMORE YOU
THEY DON'T UNDERSTAND WHY I LOVE YOU
WHY I WANT TO WRITE LOVE SONGS ABOUT YOU
HOW I WANT TO SPIT FIRE ABOUT YOU HOW
COULD I EVER DOUBT YOU?
YOU'RE SO FUCKING VEIN YOU PROBABLY THINK
THIS POEMS ABOUT YOU...DON'T YOU? YOU
FUCKING RIGHT IT IS!*

WORDS

WATERS FLOW PEACEFULLY IN HIS ARMS
TENDER KISSES FROM HEAD TO HIS CHEST WHERE
MY HEAD REST
EMBRACES ME IN PASSION
I MAY HAVE EMBRACED HIM TOO TIGHTLY FACE
TO FACE HE CAPTIVATES ME HANGING ON HIS
EVERY WORD
HIS INTELLECT IS FAR BEYOND THE REACH OF
MOST
I WILL SWALLOW HIS MENTAL GLADLY

I AM NEVER MAD

I AM NEVER MAD OVER THIS END IT WITH AN
AIR KISS LET'S NOT GET IT TWIST
I DON'T WANT TO TWIST NOTHING BUT AN L
STUFFED WITH SOME STICKY
WITH ALL THAT ISH YOU TALKING ON THE OTHER
SIDE OF THE FENCE JUST MISS ME WITH ALL THAT
YOU MAD CAUSE YOU CAN'T GET BACK SOME SAY
THAT KITTEN IS ALL THE SAME DON'T BE MISLED
IT'S THE DIFFERENCE BETWEEN A BUTTERED
BISCUIT AND DRY WHITE BREAD
SHE GOT YOU CAUGHT UP FOR A FEW MOMENTS
BUT I DON'T SWEAT ISH
SHE BETTER NOT HOLD YOU IN HIGH REGARD
YOU A FUCKIN FRAUD
I PEEPED YOUR GAME FROM THE START BUT I
WAS BORED AND DECIDED TO PLAY
SO CAME THE TIME TO MAKE YOU GO AWAY
JUST IN TIME HE STEPPED UP AND ASKED IF I
WAS DONE PLAYING GAMES
HIM HOLDING ME MADE ME FORGET YOUR NAME
HIS INTELLECT IS OFF THE CHAIN
HE LOOKS IN MY EYES AND FOR A SECOND MY
HEART STOPS
HE SAY COME HERE AND MY CLOTHES DROP

WHERE HAVE YOU BEEN ALL MY LIFE?

THIS IS MY GROUND

STAND MY GROUND THAT'S WHAT I DO
DRAW LINES IN THE SAND WHEN IT COMES TO
YOU
MY FRUSTRATION   COULD BE FEW
WITH THIS SITUATION OF ME AND YOU YOU PUSH
SHOVE THEN CLAIM LOVE YOU THROW YOUR FIST
IN THE AIR
AND EXPECT ME NOT TO CARE?
WAVED MY WHITE FLAG IN THE AIR MANY A DAY
JUST TO MAKE THE PAIN GO AWAY
YOU YELL
I CURSE
THEN WE PUT IT IN REVERSE
PERFECT FIGHTING AS IF REHEARSED
WHEN I DEMAND RESPECT THAT YOU WON'T GIVE

I AM TRIPPING
WHEN I WATCH YOUR MOVES AND YOU MAD
BECAUSE YOU SLIPPIN
ALL I WANTED WAS FOR YOU TO TAKE THAT
STICK I LIKE AND START TO DIPPING
ALL IN THIS PUDDING BUT NOT EVERYONE LIKES
PUDDING
MAYBE YOU ARE A JELLO MAN
WHATEVER YOU'RE CRAVING I JUST CAN'T
UNDERSTAND, DAMN
THOUGHT YOU WOULD KISS MY TEARS AWAY
YOU NEVER EVEN REACHED FOR MY HAD WHEN I
WALKED AWAY
THEN HAD A FUCKIN NERVE TO ASK ME TO STAY
WENT TO SLEEP ON A BED OF TEARS
WOKE UP THIS MORNING AND IT'S A NEW DAY
JUST PLEASE STAY OUT OF MY WAY

WHAT IF?

WHAT IF YOU REALLY CARED?
IF WE DARED
SHARED
COMPARED ROMANCES FROM HISTORY BOOKS TO
OURS
FIRST GLANCES SPELL BOUND
WHAT IF IT WERE ONLY ME THAT YOU DREAM OF
ME YOU HELD
ME YOU PUSHED EVERYONE AWAY FOR
WHAT IF YOU TOOK THE TIME TO LET ME MAKE
YOU HAPPY? WHAT IF?

CHANGES

GOT RID OF SOME OLD TOSSED OUT SOME NEW
HAVE TO DO ME
WHAT ELSE IS THERE TO DO?
TRIALS AND TRIBULATIONS ARE FOREVER HAD TO
PUT SOME THINGS TOGETHER SHAKE HIM OFF
KICK HIM TO THE SIDE
LET MY HAIR DOWN AND KEEP IN STRIDE LABELS
AND ASSUMPTIONS RELATIONSHIPS DYSFUNCTION
SOMETIMES CAN'T GET MY WORDS RIGHT
CONJUNCTION JUNCTION
WHAT'S HIS FUNCTION?
PLAYED SECOND BEST FOR GREAT SEX
SOMETIMES IT GOES LIKE THAT
I'M SURE SOME OF YOU REMEMBER THAT
NEW DAY, NEW SMILE, NEW DICK, NEW STYLE

FALLING

YELLING!

SCREAMING!

SHOUTING!

WHISPERING, TAKE ME AND DO WHAT YOU WILL

I HAVE NO NEED FOR MY OWN THOUGHTS

YOUR THOUGHTS ARE MY THOUGHTS

WE PULL AND TUG UNTIL WE FALL DEEP INTO LUST

RANDOM

*I try to leave and it pulls me back His wit
is unmatched by any Understanding him is
my goal
His words hurt him as well
His voice melts my anger
I walk away and his tone and position
commands my attention
I just want to make him happy*

IN MY MIND

IN MY MIND I HATE YOU
IN MY HEART I LOVE YOU
IN MY BLOOD I NEED YOU
IN MY CELLS I DON'T LIKE YOU
TWISTED WORDS
FAKE SMILES
DIRTY LOOKS ALL TO GET EVEN
WE DO THIS DANCE EACH OF US PRETENDING
WAITING FOR THE PERFECT TIME TO STRIKE
UNAWARE THAT WE BOTH HAVE REVENGE ON THE
BRAIN
ALLOW ME TO KISS AWAY YOUR PLOT AND THEN
SUM.

PARDON

PARDON MY STREET
HE IS ATTRACTED TO A SOFTER SIDE OF SPEAKING
THEY ARE SO LADY LIKE AND SWEET VERY LOW-
KEY I CALL THEM SALAD EATERS
THEY SMOKE VIRGINIA SLIMS OR BLACK AND
MILD'S ATTEMPTING TO LOOK
DAINTY
I LIKE MEAT
FROM TIME TO TIME BRING HEAT DON'T SMOKE
BUT IF NECESSARY I'LL SMOKE THAT ASS
STAYING TALKING TRASH
GOT A CANNON ON MY HIP AND HE READY TO
BLAST
THINK YOU CAN TAKE ME? BETTER MOVE FAST
YOU CAN KEEP THAT LADYLIKE SHIT
WHEN DA SHIT HIT THE FAN AIN'T NO TIME FORE
IT
HE MAY THINK MY MOUTH TO SLICK
BUT HE ALSO KNOW HOW I TREAT THE DICK

IF HE KNEW BETTER

LITTLE BOY BLUE WHAT HAPPENED TO YOU?

MY GIRL LEFT ME AND I DON'T KNOW WHAT TO
DO
SAID SHE WAS GOING OUT WITH HER GIRLS TO
HEAR SOME POETRY
CAME BACK HOME AND BARELY NOTICED ME
SAID SHE WAS ENLIGHTENED
SHE NOW DREAMS IN COLOR
OF THIS FORM OF ART SHE IS NOW A LOVER
GOT EXCITED ABOUT THE PEOPLE SHE MET
SAID SOME DUDE SPIT SOME FIYAH AND MADE
HER WET SHE HELD HER FIST IN THE AIR AND
YELLED BLACK POWER I NEED AN UMBRELLA FOR
THE VERBAL SHOWER
FOLLOWED HER ON A WEDNESDAY NIGHT
PEEPED THROUGH THE WINDOW AND MY GIRL
WAS ON THE MIC
THE THINGS SHE SAID MADE MY MANHOOD GROW
NEXT WEEK I'M IN THE FRONT ROW

IF

IF I COULD
IF HE WOULD
I WOULD KISS HIM FROM HEAD TO TOE JUST TO
LET HIM KNOW
I WOULD TELL HIM I LOVE HIM ALWAYS
I WOULD MAKE HIM LISTEN TO MY MOANS AND
GROANS AS I TELL HIM TO GO DEEPER
HE WOULD ASK WHO IT BELONGS TO AND I
WOULD TELL HIM.. YOU ALREADY KNOW
HE WOULD FEEL ME MISSING HIM IN ONE NIGHT
MY SHAME AND EMBARRASSMENT WOULD TAKE A
BACKSEAT TO HIS THRUST
I CAN TASTE HIM ON MY LIPS AND CAN'T TOUCH
HIM
HE IS IMPRINTED ON ME IN MORE WAYS THAN
ONE

MEETING HER

NAW FUCK DAT
I WANNA KNOW WHERE DIS CHICK LIVE AT
SHE KEEPS CALLING MY MAN
I CAN'T UNDERSTAND THAT
SHE AIN'T SHIT BUT A HOE
SHE BETTA ACT LIKE SHE KNOW
CALLING HIS PHONE ALL HOURS OF THE NIGHT
I DON'T GIVE A DAMN ABOUT HER BEING HIS WIFE
SHE KNOW WHAT IT IS
HE ONLY WIT HER CAUSE SHE GOT DEM KIDS
I'M A HOOD-RAT
I'LL LAY THAT BITCH FLAT
HE SMOKING MY PURPLE HAZE
LIKE A RAT IN SEARCH OF THE CHEESE, HE
RUNNING THROUGH THIS MAZE
YOU CAN HAVE HIM BACK
RIGHT AFTER WE FINISH A LITTLE OF THIS AND
WHOLE LOT OF THAT

SHADOW

I AM STANDING IN THE SHADOW OF YOU
FINDING MYSELF TALKING TO YOU AND YOU ARE
NOT THERE
I AM AFRAID TO MOVE
I KNOW YOUR SHADOW WILL SOON VANISH
YOU HAVE BEEN AWAY FOR FAR TOO LONG
I ASK QUESTIONS THAT GO UNANSWERED
I USE ALL OF MY FINGERS TO TRACE THE OUTLINE
OF YOUR SHADOW OVER AND OVER
I IMAGINE THAT YOU CAN FEEL ME AND THAT YOU
STILL CARE
I MODEL MY FAVORITE NIGHTTIME APPAREL IN
HOPES THAT YOU WILL SAY "YES THAT'S THE ONE
I LIKE"
I USE YOUR OILS AND I LAY WITH THEM EACH
NIGHT
I GAZE UPON YOUR PHOTO AND SHARE SECRETS
WITH YOU THAT GO INTO AIR
I SHOWER TO OUR FAVORITE SONG IN ORDER TO
HAVE DINNER WITH YOUR VOICE
SMALL TALK AND LAUGHTER FILL THE DIMLY LIT
ROOM AS I PRETEND THAT YOU ARE WITH ME
ALL THAT REMAINS IS YOUR SHADOW

BEING CRAZY

ITS NOT A GAME IT'S THE REASON WHY I WANT
TO SCREAM OUT HIS NAME AND PUNCH HIM IN HIS
FACE
HOW DARE HE REMAIN NAMELESS?
THE SHIT WAS DONE SO SMOOTH SHOULD HAVE
PEEPED HIS GAME AND ITS OK THOUGH
AFTER SO MANY POEMS HE IS GOING TO MAKE ME
FAMOUS
LOVE HIM SO HARD
HE HARDLY CARES
WISH FOR HIM AND HE WISHES HE WOULD HAVE
NEVER
CAN'T FORGET
HE CAN'T REMEMBER
HE MADE A DIFFERENCE
I MADE NO DIFFERENCE AT ALL
WANTED TO CONSUME HIS TIME
HE WANTED TO PASS THE TIME AWAY
CRIED IN HIM
HE CRIED FREEDOM
A MID SUMMER'S NIGHT
THE VERY DARK NIGHT
DOO WOP CAN'T HOLD THE CORNER BECAUSE WE
DO
HE SLOWLY TURNS AND WALKS INTO THE NIGHT
I HATE HIS ASS!

US BE

LIKE HIM BUT HATE HIM
WON'T MALLY BUT DATE HIM
ON A SCALE FROM ONE TO TEN STILL CAN'T RATE
HIM
SO FAR FROM SOFT DON'T MISTAKE HIM
PUSH YOUR LUCK IF YOU THINK YOU CAN TAKE
HIM
I'M THE ONLY ONE THAT CAN BREAK HIM
LOVE TOO STRONG I TRIED TO ESCAPE HIM
HIS LOVE IS A LANGUAGE I WANT TO TRANSLATE
HIM MELODIES SUIT ROUND US OFF KEY WE
SOMETIMES BE TWO LEFT FEET WITH BOTH TRYING
TO LEAD
BUMPED HEADS NOW WE BLEED
HIS SWEAT STINGS MY OPEN AS CAR AND BUMS
YET FEELS SO SOOTHING TO ME

THIS THING

THIS THING
MY HEART SINGS
THIS SOUND
RINGS IN MY PRIVATE PLACES
THAT POSSIBILITY OF US
WANT IT SO MUCH
SUCKING ELBOWS AND TOES
ANYTHING GOES WITH EACH TWIST MAKE A WISH
ALLOW ME PASSAGE ON THIS TRIP
MY SOFT LIPS TAKE SIPS OF YOU ALL NIGHT
WATCH ME FRIGHT TO KEEP FROM EXPLODING
HOLD ME THROUGH MY TREMBLE
COACH ME THROUGH CONTINUOUS SESSIONS

COULD CARE LESS

HE DOESN'T CARE IF I MISS HIM
HIS VOICE AND LETTERS ACROSS MY SCREEN FADE
QUICKLY
PULL ME IN TO PULL AWAY BUT I AM LEARNING
FAST MY FANTASY OF HIM IS FLAWLESS AND
PERFECT UNBLEMISHED IS HIS REPUTATION WITHIN
MY DREAMS

SHADOW BOXING

SWIFT JABS
TOE TO TOE IN THE MIDDLE OF THE RING
WE BOTH ATTEMPT TO DUCK
HITS FLY BY AS WE WAIT FOR AN OPENING
FANCY FOOT WORK JUST TO GET TANGLED UP
ANYWAY
WE RETREAT TO OUR RESPECTABLE CORNERS AND
RECHARGE
SWING AFTER SWING NO REF IN SIGHT
WHO WILL FALL?
LOW BLOWS COME IN A RUSH
WE HAVE LONG WALKED AWAY AND ALL THAT
STANDS ARE OUR SHADOWS

DREAMING

IN MY SLUMBER I TALK TO HIM
WE HAVE BREAKFAST BY THE WINDOW AND
WATCH THE SUNRISE
IN THE EVENING WE WATCH IT SET AND MAKE
PLANS
HE WANTS A MOVIE AND I WANT DANCING
HE TAKES ME DANCING BUT WE CAN'T STAY TOO
LONG
THEY HAVE PLAYED ONE TOO MANY JAMS
RUSHING HOME WE FALL IN THE DOOR
TEASING I TELL HIM..READ ME ONE OF YOUR
POEMS FIRST
WITHOUT A BIT OF HESITATION
HE OPENS HIS MOUTH AND I HANG ON EVERY
WORD
NO LONGER ABLE TO CONTAIN MY ENERGY
I CAN FEEL HIS BREATH ON MY LIPS AND THEN...I
AWAKE

COFFEE WITH GOD

TODAY I SEE YOU BOUGHT THE CLOUDS OUT
IT'S A LITTLE TOO CHILLY FOR MY TASTE BUT IF
YOU LIKE IT I LOVE IT
DID I EVER TELL YOU ABOUT THE TIME THAT I.
WELL I GUESS YOU KNOW ABOUT THAT!
I MADE FOOD ON THAT PROMISE BUT I FELL
SHORT OF THAT OTHER THING. DID YOU FORGIVE
ME FOR THAT?
SOO HOW HAVE YOU BEEN WITH ALL THE WARS,
FAMINE, POLITICS, PRAYERS, DEATHS BIRTHS, FIRES,
FLOODS, EARTHQUAKES AND ALL OF THE OTHER
THINGS GOING ON
I MEANT TO ASK YOU HOW YOU MANAGED TO
TAKE CARE OF ALL OF THOSE THINGS AND STILL
CARE FOR
ME?
ANYWAY THANK YOU FOR MY FAMILY, FRIENDS, A
JOB, SOME WRITING SKILLS, AND LOVE
THANK YOU FOR MY CHILDREN, HUSBAND, AND MY
GRANDCHILD. THANK YOU FOR ALLOWING ME TO
BE ME.
OH I SEE YOU HAVE FINISHED YOUR COFFEE
THANKS FOR STOPPING BY
(LOOKING INTO GODS COFFEE CUP)
WOW WHO KNEW GOD LIKED HIS COFFEE BLACK?
THEN AGAIN WHY WOULDN'T HE

WHAT'S IN A DAY?

*WHAT A DIFFERENCE A DAY MAKES HEARTS ONCE
HELD TOGETHER SO STRONG DRIFT ALONG TAKING
ON WATER DAMAGE WATCHING WHAT ONCE WAS
SEEMS SAD ONCE BRIGHT WITH LUSTER
NOW DARK AND BROKEN BE CAREFUL NOT TO
TOUCH SPLINTERS AWAIT*

MY PRAYER

HEAVENLY FATHER, PLEASE FORGIVE ME FOR
COMING TO YOU LIKE THIS
A BITCH IS PISSED
SORRY FOR USING VULGARITY
I NEED SOME CHARITY
TRYING TO MAINTAIN AND BE A GOOD GIRL BEING
A GOOD GIRL MAKES ME WANT TO VOMIT VOMIT
UP SHIT FROM YESTERDAY
THINKING ABOUT YESTERYEAR
WHEN I USED TO ROCK MY COUSINS GEAR
I WANT TO SPIT VENOM AT THOSE BITCHES FROM
BACK THEN
PLEASE FORGIVE ME FOR MY SHORT COMINGS AND
FOR FALLING SHORT OF YOUR MERCY
AND MOST OF ALL...
THANK YOU FOR ALLOWING ME TO SEE MY
ENEMIES FALL

DEAR GOD

DEAR GOD IN CASE WE NEVER MEET PROTECT ME
WHEN I SLEEP
KEEP MY ENEMIES AWAY
I WILL SEE THEM AGAIN SOMEDAY
FORGIVE ME FOR VERY SELDOM PICKING UP YOUR
BOOK
I KNOW THAT'S NOT A GOOD LOOK I GOT ON
BENDED KNEE TO PRAY SORRY FOR FORGETTING
WHAT TO SAY I FEEL SO LOST AND
MISUNDERSTOOD
ALL I REALLY WANTED TO DO IS BRING THE
WORLD SOME GOOD
AT TIMES I AM SWEET AS PIE
OTHER TIMES THE LOOK OF DEATH IN MY EYE
PICKED UP THAT THIN AND STARTED TO BLAST
FELT LIKE I WAS HAVING SPASMS
ADDICTED TO THE GUN POWDER NO HAVING
ORGASMS
I WANT TO BREAK FREE FROM THIS LIFE OF SIN
MY SKINK MY SMOKES AND A BOTTLE OF GIN
BREAKING FREE BUT IT PULLS ME BACK IN

UNTITLED

*I FEEL YOUR ENERGY AS I THINK OF YOU
IMAGINING WE ARE SHARING THE SAME SPACE AT
THIS MOMENT
INHALING ALL OF YOU AND CARRYING YOU WITH
ME
YOUR VOICE GETS ME HIGH I WANT YOU SO BAD...
COME HERE*

BLACK QUEEN

BEAUTY IN MANY SHADES OF EARTH
LIFE GIVING TO THIS UNIVERSE
ALL MANKIND BIRTHED BY HERE
COLOR OF CHOCOLATE, CARAMEL, ALMOND KINGS
BOW TO HER FEET
QUALITIES OF ALL THINGS ROYAL UNIQUE IN
EVERY WAY EVERLASTING THROUGHOUT TIME
ENVIOUS OF HER BEAUTY OTHER CULTURES ARE
NEVER UNDERESTIMATE HER POWER

THIS HURT

THIS PAIN IS A WINDOW TO MY EXISTENCE
YOU CREATED THIS WINDOW AND PAINTED THE
FRAME
YOU PAINTED THE SADNESS IN MY EYES AND THE
DESPAIR IN MY SOUL
YET ON THE OTHER SIDE THE SUN SHINES

BETWEEN

BETWEEN ME AND YOU I LIKE WHAT YOU DO
DARK SKIES BLUE HARD STINGING RAIN TOO SOFT
SEXY DEW
MY DO WAS TIGHT UNTIL THAT NIGHT
ONCE MAY HAVE BEEN WRONG
BUT BECAME JUST RIGHT
SOFT LIPS TASTE OF WINE
I COULD NEVER HANDLE MY SPIRITS

YOU COULD ALWAYS HANDLE MY SPIRIT

HANDS ON MY HIPS!

*I PUT MY HANDS ON MY HIPS AT TIMES BECAUSE
THEY HOLD THE WEIGHT OF THE WORLD*

*BACK ON THE MASTERS PLANTATION I HAD YOU
ON MY HIP, A BASKET ON MY HEAD AND THAT
WHITE BABY ON MY BACK*

*IN EGYPT I PUT MY HANDS ON MY HIPS TO
ALLOW MY SERVANTS TO ADORN ME WITH THE
FINEST JEWELS*

*IN THE 50'S AND 60'S I PUT MY HANDS ON MY
HIPS TO REST THEM AFTER A DAY OF PROTESTING
FOR THE RIGHTS OF MY PEOPLE*

*AS A BIKE NEEDS HANDLEBARS AND A STEERING
WHEEL NEEDS A CAR
MY HIPS ARE PERFECT FOR HOLDING ON TO*

*YESTERDAY I PUT MY HANDS ON MY HIPS TO
KEEP FROM SLAPPING THE SHIT OUT OF YOU FOR
FEEDING ME THAT LIE ABOUT THAT CHICK*

*FINALLY I AS A BLACK WOMAN PUT MY HANDS
ON MY HIPS TO HELP ME BIRTH MANKIND AND WE
DID!*

THANK YOU

HE BE ALRIGHT SOMETIMES BUT HE REALLY AIN'T
SHIT
HE SO UNDERSTANDING AT TIMES WHEN HE IS
NOT BEING FAKE
HIS SMILE IS SO WARM AND INVITING UNTIL YOU
REALIZE THAT HE IS NOT LOOKING AT YOU
YOU ARE PISSED BECAUSE HE IS HAPPY WITHOUT
YOU
THEN REALIZING YOUR OWN SELFISHNESS YOU
FEEL SORRY FOR HIM AND KEEP IT MOVING
EVERYONE MAKES MISTAKES
IT'S WHAT YOU LEARN FROM THOSE MISTAKES
AND THE KNOWLEDGE YOU GAIN
I HAVE LEARNED A LOT FROM HIM
I GUESS I SHOULD THANK HIM FOR BREAKING MY
HEART

THANK YOU

SHALL WE DANCE?

THE EXIT SIGN BECAME MY REFUGE OR SO I
THOUGHT
HE INVITED ME FOR ONE LAST DANCE
I TRY TO MIMIC HIS STEPS
AS HE IN TURNS TRIES TO MATCH MY BODY
MOVEMENT
FINALLY A MOTION SO SUPERB
RIVERS BEGIN TO RUN
LIFE PRESERVERS UNAVAILABLE
NO CHOICE BUT TO RIDE IT OUT
HOPEFULLY WE DON'T CRASH AGAINST THE ROCKS

GIVER OF LIFE

GIVER OF LIFE
PROVIDING LIFE'S LESSONS
EXPRESSIONS OF LOVE
BROWN SKINNED GODDESS
HIPS BARING GIFTS UNTO HIM
ON BENDED KNEES PRAYING FOR SAFE TRANSITION
INTO THIS WORLD
BLACK BEAUTY ON BENDED KNEE PRAYING FOR
TRANSITION INTO THE NEXT LIFE FOR HER SEEDS

I ADORE YOU MOMMY

JUST IN TIME

I GAVE UP ON THINGS THAT ARE SOMEWHAT
NECESSARY
PLANTING A TREE TO STIMULATE ME CREATING A
WORLD OF POSITIVE EXCHANGE MY LYRICAL HERO
MY SUPERNATURAL SAVIOR
VERSATILE VERSES TO FIT MY MOOD SWINGS
PASSION POEMS BECAUSE HE HAS PICKED UP ON
MY SOFT SIDE AND HOLDS IT DELICATELY
WONDERLAND OF WORDS
I AM ENTRANCED
MAGIC CARPET RIDE

GOODBYE

WATCHING THE NIGHT TURN INTO DAY
ASSUMING YOU ARE THINKING OF ME BECAUSE MY
MIND IS ON YOU
THE W'S GOT ME BLUE
WANTING WISHING WAITING WILLING ALL FOR YOU
MY MIND HAS NOT BEEN MY OWN FOR SOME TIME
NOW
I FEEL ITS TIME TO PUT THIS THING TO BED
GOODNIGHT AS IN GOODBYE

ALL OR NOTHING

MY MINDSET IS A PUZZLE HATE IT OR LOVE IT
CONTINUING TO SOUL SEARCH
SEARCHING THE GALAXIES FOR A PIECE AND A
PEACE OF ME
LAYERS TO ME PHYSICALLY AND MENTALLY
CONSTRUCTED BY THE MOST HIGH ENLIGHTENED
BY MANY
SOMETIMES RAGE AGAINST THE MACHINE
LOVE YOU WITH ALL OF MY BEING
EXPECT THE SAME BUT RESPECT THE GAME
MY MAN STRAPPED I'M DOING
I'M DOWN WITH THAT
IF I DESERVED TO BE SLAPPED YOU GETTING
SLAPPED BACK THAT JUST HOW I DO
TAKE CHARGE BUT NEVER MIND A MAN THAT
ASSUMES THE POSITION
MY THING IS LIKE THAT
PLAY MY PART FROM THE WORK FORCE TO THE
KITCHEN
I'M COMPLICATED NOT TWO HANDFULS BUT THREE
NO NEED TO APPLY FOR A POSITION IF YOU CAN'T
DEAL WITH ME

POETRY IS IN ME

WORDS ARE POWERFUL THEY SAY WHAT I CAN'T

THEY TELL SECRETS THAT YOU TRY TO HIDE

THEY MAKE YOU LAUGH, CRY, YELL, AND EVEN MAKE WAR

LOVE OR WAR, I MAKE MUSIC...YOU DECIDE

SLOW DOWN

SHE LOVED HIM TOO MUCH TOO SOON

HE ACCEPTED TOO FAST

HE PLAYED AND TOYED

SHE FELL AND COULD NOT STAND

SHE WORE HER HEART ON· SLEEVE

HE TOOK THE SHIRT TO THE CLEANERS

SHE PUSHED THE LOVE ENVELOPE

HE ADDRESSED IT, RETURN TO SENDER

SHE COULD FEEL HIM LIGHT YEARS AWAY
WAITING FOR THE DAY
FANTASIES BEGIN TO CONTROL HER EVERY
MOMENT

SHE MUST LEARN TO BOTTLE THEM AND PUT
THEM TO THE SIDE

SHE CAN'T CONTINUE TO DREAM
KISSES FROM HIM MELT INTO AIR
HIS WHISPERS OF LOVE ARE NOW APPRECIATED
BY SOMEONE ELSE

SHE MUST TAKE THIS HARSH REALITY AND ALLOW
WHAT WAS TO GIVE HER COMFORT

UNTITLED

HE TELLS ME HIS SECRETS
I WHISPER MY FANTASY
WE ENTRANCE ONE ANOTHER
NIGHTS ON END WE DELIGHT IN WE TWO
HIS PEN ERECT
MY PAPER AWAITS TO BE WRITTEN ON FOR ALL
ETERNITY WITH HIS NAME

Just me

I am sweet past honey
I give all that I have and then some
Rider til the wheels fall off and build a
better bike
My 9–5 does me just fine
Sweet sour
Smooth rough
Once you get a taste you hurt yourself to
give it up
No one wants to be hooked on drugs
Some have no choice
Out of my reach you may do just fine But
once within the sound of my voice That ass
is mine
Think back to a childhood bumped and
bruised learning how to ride a bike
You throw your hands into the air ready
to declare defeat
You know that I'm so worth it once our
eyes meet

WINTER LOVE

SMALL WHITE CLOUDS FALL FROM THE SKY
LAYER THE GROUND
WE MAKE SNOW ANGELS IN WINTER WHITE
NOW WE LET HOT CHOCOLATE WITH SMALL
WHITE CLOUDS SLIDE DOWN OUR THROATS
IN FRONT OF THE FIRE PLACE
THOUGHT PROVOKED
CLIMB INTO BED
MY BODY WARMS YOU
IT HEATS US AS YOU GROW
LONG GONE IS THE SNOW FROM YOUR EMOTIONS
NO SOUND INVADES OUR SPACE EXCEPT THE
MOANING AND PANTING BETWEEN THE TWO OF US
WE ARE OUR OWN SNOW GLOBE GETTING LOST IN
WINTER LOVE
WITH WINTER AROUND US WE MAKE BROWN
BABIES

SHADOW MAN

MY EYES FIXED ON THE SHADOW
FEELING HIS EVERY BREATH ON THE BACK OF MY
SHOULDER
HE KISSED MY LIPS PUSHING HIS WAY TO INVADE
MY MOUTH
I SLOWLY INHALE HIS OFFERING
WE STAND IN LINE US FEW
EACH WITH DIFFERENT OFFERINGS IN HAND
HE WATCHES WITH EYES OF AN EAGLE TO
MOVEMENTS MADE
I FEEL HIM THOUGH HE IS NOT THERE
MY INNER QUIVERS AS MY OUTER SHELL REFLECTS
NOTHING
MADNESS OR MAGIC ALLOWS HIM POSSESSION
OVER MY MIND BODY AND SOUL
HIS VOICE SOFT YET THUNDEROUS IN HIS WRATH
NEEDING HIM IN EVER WAY POSSIBLE WAY
BECOMES MY TORTURED DAYS AND NIGHT
LONGING TO GAZE UPON A POSSIBILITY THAT DOES
NOT EXIST
ARMS REACHING FOR HIM THIGHS BEGGING FOR
HIM VOICE CRYING FOR HIM
TOUCHING MYSELF IN MY PRETEND LOVE MAKING
SESSIONS WITH HIM
GIVING ME JUST ENOUGH TO KEEP ME GOING
HE WALKS FROM THE SHADOW TO DISAPPEAR
MY MENTAL BLOSSOMS LIKE THE MAY FLOWER
AFTER AN APRIL SHOWER BECAUSE OF HIM
ATTEMPTS TO TURN AND LOOK AWAY IS BEING
UNTRUE TO MYSELF

DAYDREAMS

DAYDREAMS OF EVOLUTIONARY ESCAPADES
WITH YOU IN MIND
KEEPING ME MENTALLY AND PHYSICALLY
ENTRANCED
UNTIL MY THIRD EYE IS BLIND
REFUGE FROM YOUR CHARISMA IS UNDERSTOOD TO
BE NON EXISTING IN THIS WORLD OR THE NEXT
I WANT TO MAKE LOVE TO YOUR SOUL
IT AIN'T ABOUT THE SEX BUT IF YOU GIVE IT TO
ME I PROMISE TO GIVE IT BACK
WE CAN TALK POLITICS, RELIGION
EDUCATION   RIGHT NOW I NEED FOR YOU TO
TEACH ME
I PROMISE TO GIVE STUDENT PARTICIPATION
YES I AM QUEEN AND YES I NEED A KING BUT
RIGHT
DAMN NOW ALL I NEED IS...THAT THING THAT
THING (IN MY BEST LAUREN
HILL VOICE)

SKY WATCHER

Looking up at how the clouds play tag
Watching the sun play peek a boo
The wind kisses my lips and caresses my skin
Like a child I play roller coaster out of
the window with my hand
I turn and look to him only to see the man
he used to be
I remember those special places and times
Damn, just when I thought I knew
I really didn't know

They Don't Understand

They don't understand why I want you as
my man
When I'm low you pick me up and help me
to understand
When I feel I can't smile you bring the sun
When my metaphors make no sense what so
ever
I have you and...
You're always on my mind

THIS DANCE WE DO

MEMORIES OF YOU INVADE MY SPACE
I AM TAKEN TO ANOTHER TIME AND PLACE
AND YOU'RE NO WHERE TO BE FOUND
I'M TOUCHING YOU AND YOU ARE TOUCHING ME
MY NIGHTS OF PASSION MY SHEETS WET WITH US
ALL NIGHT
STILL YOUR NO WHERE TO BE FOUND

SECRETS

*I FELT HE OPENED MY HEART AND TOLD MY
INNER THOUGHTS IN HIS VERSES
AND MAYBE I JUST THINK TOO HIGHLY OF MYSELF
THAT HE WOULD EVEN GIVE OUR SHIT A SECOND
THOUGHT
HE MAKES ME FEEL LIKE A YORK PEPPERMINT
PATTI
STANDING ON A HOT BEACH WITH COLD WAVES
SPLASHING ALL OVER MY BODY AS JELLY FISH
NIBBLE ON MY TOES
I AM SO SORRY I WANTED TO WATCH CASINO
WHILE YOU WERE IN YOUR SCAR-FACE BAG*

BABY ROCK

*I ROCK MYSELF TO SLEEP AT NIGHT BECAUSE I
NEED TO FEEL THAT RHYTHM
THE SLOW ROTATION OF MOVEMENT THAT MAKES
ME HIGH
I MISS BEING IN MY MOTHER'S BELLY WHERE IT
WAS SAFE
I WAS PROTECTED FROM HARM
HER SINGING SOFTLY AND READING STORIES IN
THE NIGHT
I MISS THAT ROCK AT NIGHT*

NO MORE US

MY WORDS ARE POURING OUT
HIS CUP NOT RECEIVING
HE IS NO LONGER THIRSTY
EVEN IF CRAWLING THROUGH THE DESERT HE
WOULD NOT DRINK
TOO PAINFUL FOR MY
MENTAL TO GRASP
I ATTEMPT TO RETURN
HURT WITH HURT BUT HE DOES NOT CARE
LONG FORGOTTEN IS MY LAUGH AND SMILE
NO WORRIES IN REGARDS TO NIGHTS OF I LOVE
YOU AND PASSION
SMILES REPAINTED IN NEW COLORS
JUST WANTING TO REMEMBER HIS BREATH

STRANGER THAN FICTION

*I AM DRAWN TO THE WORD PLAY THAT IS JUST
OUT OF REACH*

*I HEAR YOUR WORDS DEEP DOWN BENEATH
CURIOUS ENERGY PLAYS UP AND DOWN MY SPINE
WHILE OUR FLOWS INTERTWINE*

*I WANT A POETIC ORGASM
I WANT A POETIC EXCHANGE
I WANT A POETIC SULTRY FLOW
I WANT TO FEEL IT GROW*

*IT'S STRANGE I DON'T EVEN KNOW THE WHO,
WHAT, WHERE
AND RIGHT NOW I DON'T EVEN CARE
COME FLOW WITH ME*

I GOT THE POINT

DESPITE HOW I FEEL DADDY
I WILL KEEP IT REAL DADDY
WOULDN'T KNOW THE TRUTH IF IT SMACKED YOU
IN YOUR FACE YES POLICING ALL DAY FOR WHAT
I THOUGHT WAS MINE
THIS FUCKED UP RELATIONSHIP GOT ME DOING
TIME
ABUSE GIVES YOU NOT?
A SECOND AGO YOU COULDN'T GET ENOUGH
YOU USE LOVE THE CUFFS
SAID YOU LIKED IT ROUGH NOW IS IT TOO MUCH?
SHOULD HAVE KNOWN NOT TO TRUST
FROM THE BEGINNING TO THE END OF US
LET'S NO LONGER DISCUSS

ON HIS TOP

*He got that bring that ass here affect on
me
You ain't going nowhere tonight
I'm smiling like yeah you right
He ain't stressing or sweating no other man
Because they can't put it down like he can
One word and he got me at attention
His shit is smooth in case I forgot to
mention
Wrapped around his little finger
I know my place
Right up in his face
She had a place in his past
But she left him up for grabs
I'm trying to snatch up all of him
Put him on my team
Doing whatever he likes on some sex
machine*

BETTER JUDGMENT

MY MIND SAYS YES AND YET YOU TRY TO DENY
IT OF KNOWING
THE EXTRA SENSES SAY WAKE UP! BUT I BUILD
ROADBLOCKS
SOMETIMES WE BUILD WITHOUT TRULY HAVING A
FLOOR PLAN
WE TAKE CHANCES AND RISK IT ALL FOR LOVE
SAKE
WHY SHOULD I TRY ANYMORE?
BECAUSE GOD IS LOVE AND WE WERE CREATED
IN HIS IMAGE
CALL ME MOTHER NATURE

SAVE HER

DESTINY HAS SIDELINED THE HEART
SADNESS FILLS HER EXISTENCE FOR THE TIME
BEING
HER POT OF GOLD AT THE END OF THE RAINBOW
HAS BEEN STOLEN ALONG WITH HER UNICORN AND
SINGING HARP

HER FREE SPIRIT HAS BEEN CAGED FOR NOW AND
SHE ONLY SINGS SONGS BY
BILLIE HOLIDAY, SO YOU REALLY CAN'T TELL IF
SHE IS HAPPY OR SAD
SHE HAS MEMORIZED THE WORDS TO GOOD
MORNING
HEARTACHE ONLY TODAY IS WEDNESDAY

HER KNIGHT RIDING HIS WHITE HORSE THAT
SHOULD HAVE BEEN COMING TO RESCUE HER HAS
TAKEN A DETOUR AND CAN'T BE FOUND
LOST AND TURNED OUT SHE FEELS.. CALL HER
OLIVIA

So Bad

It's been so long
Touch me there
Hell yes I'm scared
I have taken enough trash to fill a
garbage truck
Now you ready to fuck Take your time
with me Ease me into freakdom
Make me the only royal subject in your
kingdom
Show me the ways of your land
Put me in the position to want no other
man
Connect status all a go
If I shake. I am enjoying it in It's just the
rapture you bring It's making my body sing
I won't let go
I can feel you grow I'm nervous baby
Oh my..

RED MOON

High moon once appeared white from a far
Now seems red amongst the stars Red,
dipped in blood of many Surrounded   by
our tears
Screams and cries for help
Married and shared against our will
Our youth spilled
Our innocence torn from our bodies and
left on display
We hold our breath afraid to make a
sound
Our families cry out in protest and beat
themselves
We cry and wait in line to be beaten,
abused, molested, and killed
Some color hands that should be helping us
are hurting us
Help Us! Help Us!
We are your daughters!

WAITING FOR FOREVER

I WAIT AND HE SPEAKS
NOT UNDERSTANDING THE VERBAL OF IT ALL I
ASK HIM TO BREAK DOWN M3EANINGS
LAUGHING HE EXPRESSES HIMSELF AND THOUGH HE
DOESN'T SPEAK A WORD I OVER-STAND EVERY
WORK
BECOMING TONGUE TIED FROM HARD KISSES
INHALING EVERY BIT OF HIM IN EVERY WAY
FEELING MY MENTAL SUDDENLY OPEN UP AND
BECOME MORE EXPOSED THAN I EVER COULD
HAVE IMAGINED
DISCOVERING MY HIDDEN SECRETS AND BREAKING
THROUGH THE WALL THAT I HAD
RECENTLY FRAMED
STRANGE HAPPENINGS
FEELING THE NEED TO TURN AWAY BECAUSE IT
WAS TOO GOOD TO BE TRUE USUALLY IS JUST
THAT
AFRAID TO TURN AND WALK AWAY
AFRAID TO MOVE ANY CLOSER
HE COMES INTO ME AND I HAVE NO CHOICES BUT
TO LAY IT ALL ON THE LINE

VOICES WITHIN

HIS VOICE HAS BECOME MY INSTANT ORGASM THAT
I NEED EACH DAY
I AM LONELY WITHOUT IT
BECOMING FIXED ON HIS EYES AND LIPS I WOULD
GIVE ALMOST ANYTHING TO BE NEAR THEM NOW
HIS SCENT IS BEGINNING TO FADE AND IS TAKING
SOME OF ME WITH HIM
I TRY NOT TO SCRATCH OR SHAKE FROM MISSING
MY FIX
MY EMOTIONS ON OVERLOAD
MY MENTAL ON OVERLOAD
BECOMING AS TRANSPARENT AS A SNOW-GLOBE

KNOW ME

WOULD YOU KNOW ME IF ALL YOU HAD TO GO
ON WAS MY HEART BEAT? COULD YOU PICK MY
KISS FROM A THOUSAND KISSES?
CAN YOU HOLD MY HAND AND KNOW THAT'S IT'S
A PERFECT FIT? I KNOW YOU AND ALL OF YOUR
IMPERFECTIONS.
I KISS YOUR LIPS AND BECOME CONSUMED AND
TIPSY
I SMELL YOU AND FEEL LIFTED BEYOND THIS
WORLD

WHO ARE YOU?

WHO ARE YOU TO ACT AS IF I DON'T EXISTS
COULDN'T HAVE IMAGINED THIS TWIST
WE HAVE SHARE SO MANY COUNTLESS NIGHTS OF
CONVERSATIONS ABOUT ANYTHING AND NOTHING
I NEEDED TO BE PROTECTED AND YOU WERE
THERE I CRIED AND MY TEARS MELTED UPON
YOUR LIPS WHO ARE YOU TO TELL ME THAT
THEY WERE FAKE? TELL ME THAT IT WAS ALL
PART OF YOUR GAME
TELL ME YOU TREATED ALL OF YOUR WOMEN THE
SAME?
TOOK TIME FOR OTHER ISSUES THAT MEANT THE
WORLD TOME
MAKE ME BELIEVE IT WAS ALL A DREAM
NIGHTS LOCKED BEHIND MY BEDROOM DOOR
HAD ME DOWN ON ALL FOURS BEGGING FOR MORE
NOT ANSWERING THE DOOR FOR INTERRUPTIONS
OKAY SO MY FATHER LEFT HOME WHEN I WAS
VERY YOUNG SO HELL YES I HAVE DADDY ISSUES
STILL DON'T CHANGE THE FACT THAT I MISS YOU
YOU HAVE NO ONE TO BLAME BUT YOURSELF
BEING NICE TO ME IS NOT ENOUGH
FEELING BAD BECAUSE THIS PIECE STARTED OUT
RIGHT BUT QUICKLY WENT LEFT
THOUGHT I HAD GOLD BECAUSE IT GLITTERED
SO YES I'M A LITTLE BITTER

MY DRUG

MY DRUG OF CHOICE
WEED MAKES ME SILLY AND HUNGRY
TOO AFRAID OF NEEDLES TO SHOOT UP ANYTHING
MY NOSE I USE TO SMELL SWEET SCENTS AND
BLOWING DUE TO COLDS
SO NO CHANCE OF ME SNORTING ANY POWDER

YOU ARE MY CHOICE OF DRUG

I INHALE YOU AND BECOME SWALLOWED WITH
SILLY, SCARED, NERVOUS, AND EXCITED TO MY
TOES
I LOOK FOR YOU IN THE DARK ON MY HANDS
AND KNEES AFRAID THAT I HAVE LOST YOU
MY BLOOD IS BECOMING TOO COOL
WHERE ARE YOU

MY DRUG OF CHOICE IS YOU

MOTHER'S DAY PRAYER

HER SKIN IS THE SAME COLOR AS YOURS
SHE HAS NOT YET TASTED THE FRUIT OF
CHILDHOOD ONLY TO BE THRUST INTO A WOMAN'S
ROLE
LOOK AT HER AND SEE HER INNOCENCE
HER LAUGHTER HAS BEEN CUT OFF
HER JOY HAS TURNED BLACK AS NIGHT
FAMILIES LINE THE STREET IN PROTEST IN FEAR IN
PAIN
A MOTHER CHILD HAS BEEN RIPPED FROM HERE
HEART FROM HER ARMS
HEAR HER PLEADING, BEGGING, AND PRAYING
YOU ONCE STOOD AS A CHILD
YOU MUST REMEMBER THE SOUND OF CHILDREN
LAUGHING
PLEASE STOP THIS TORTURE
STOP THIS PERSECUTION
THEY HAVE DONE NO INJUSTICE AGAINST ANYONE
GIVE THE MOTHER'S THEIR DAUGHTERS ON THIS
MOTHER'S DAY

LITTLE COUSIN

LOOKING IN YOUR EYES I SEE SO MUCH PAIN
FROM MEMORY

I SEE SO MUCH POTENTIAL IN WHAT COULD AND
SHOULD BE

I AM OFTEN FILLED WITH ADMIRATION

YOU BEING WHO YOUR ARE EXPERE4NCE AND
STYLE ARE OF YOUR DAILY ATTIRE

AWAITING PATIENTLY FOR YOUR TURN IN THE SUN

IF THAT TIME DOES NOT COME TO YOU YOUR
PERSONALITY WILL OFTEN GO TO IT

YOUNG OLD HEAD WITH THE APPRECIATION FOR
LIFE

NEVER WALKING INTO A GUNFIGHT WITH NOTHING
BUT A KNIFE

I LAUGH TO MYSELF WHEN I HEAR YOUR TAKE ON
SITUATIONS

YOU SEEM TO HAVE BEEN A SLAVE TO YOUR OWN MENTAL AND NOW YOU SEEK RETRIBUTIONS

PHILLY

HATE IT OR LOVE IT

MY CITY MY BABY MY LOVE CRUEL AT TIMES

SO HARSH FOR NO REASON

EVERYTHING I AM OR WILL BE IS PARTLY DUE TO YOU

YOU HAVE SHOWN ME LOVE BROKE MY HEART, REJUVENATED MY SOUL

FORCED ME TO TAKE NO PRISONERS

HELD ME CAPTIVE

BIRTHED ME, MADE ME, SHOOK ME, AND WILL UNLEASH MY FULL POTENTIAL IN 2014

LET'S RIDE

PRISON WALLS

I Inhale freedom
I exhale Prison
These bars don't hold my spirit
These walls that echo
Hurt, pain, frustration, agony, and injustice
Soon will crumble beneath my feet
I will walk away with mental baggage in
my soul
I will walk away with a few scars
Nothing keeps me from wanting to be free

THIS GAME OF LOVE OR LIKE

BLUE SKIES PAINTED WITH WHITE POWDER PUFFS,
GREEN GRASS WITH BLADES TIPPED WITH MORNING
DEW
THE SUN HIGH YET PLEASANT WITH JUST THE
RIGHT AMOUNT OF WARMTH
AT THAT MOMENT NEITHER YOU, NOR I CAN
REFUSE THE ENERGY BETWEEN US
SHE CREPT INTO A CRAWL SPACE WHERE I DID
NOT EXIST
REALIZING MY MISTAKE I IMMEDIATELY OCCUPIED
EVERY ASPECT OF YOUR INTELLECT
CONSIDER MY WHISPERS TREMORS SHE IS LOST
AND CONFUSED
ATTEMPTING TO PINPOINT THE VERY MOMENT
THAT YOU AND I BECAME AN US OR A WE
SOMETIMES AN UNFORTUNATE GAME THIS
RELATIONSHIP THING
BE CAREFUL WHAT YOU WISH FOR SOMETIMES
TREACHERY MAKES NO SOUND WHAT GOES
AROUND COMES AROUND RACERS ARE YOU READY
AT THE GATE
WORD TO OLE GIRL... CHECKMATE

YOUR LOVE LETTER

TELLING HER HOW DEEP YOUR LOVE WAS

SHARING SMILES BETWEEN YOU

PLUCKED AT HEART STRINGS LIKE A HARPS SAD MELODY

WISHES ON STARS THAT I WISHED WOULD CRASH AND BURN INTO ORBIT

FELT

WHO KNEW?

NOW THAT WE ARE A THING OF THE PAST
NOW THAT WE ARE BEYOND THAT
CAN I TRULY SAY WHAT I FEEL?
CAN I LET YOU KNOW THAT I KNEW YOU DIDN'T
REALLY LOVE MY ASS? I THINK YOU LOVED
GRIPPING MY ASS
CAN I TELL YOU A SECRET AND PRAY THAT YOU
DON'T GET OFFENDED
ALL THAT I LOVED ABOUT YOU FLOATED INTO
THE AIR AND LANDED ON A CLOUD SOMEPLACE
FOR SOME POOR UNFORTUNATE SOUL TO BARE.
MY BLIND AMBITION ON MAKING YOU MINE HAD
ME LYING TO MYSELF AS WELL AS FRIENDS
YOU COULD NEVER BE MINE
JUST AS THE LION AND THE BEAR REALIZED THAT
THEY COULD NOT LIVE TOGETHER
THEY AS WE UNDERSTAND NATURE AND THAT'S
STRONGER THAN WE COULD HAVE EVER OF BEEN.
NATURE PUT US TOGETHER AND NATURE PULLED
US APART

The Take Over

He be on his poetic flow domination
I want him in heavy slow rotation
I feel him vibrating through the microphone
Imagining that we are all alone
Sometimes I need a dictionary just to keep
up with his word play
I feel his energy each day
Makes a point and stretches out his hands
Women fall like grains of sand
Through an hour glass
Intelligent, intellectual when he is in that
zone
Yet all I want to do is take him home
Fixing my eyes on his lips
See him forming words yet nothing comes
out
I be so focused on his mouth Then traveled
down south Light low
Candles lit
I just want to slip and fall on his dick
I love his poetic shit

A POET'S KISS

*A poet's kiss is divine in words and dipped
in sound
Let letters roll off of your tongue and
fall gently into my lap
As we do a verbal dance and become a
verse
Let verses become flows Uncontrolled and
untamed Let them run free and wild
Play with me from A to Z and lets just B*

PLEASE LET ME EXPLAIN

IT WAS STUPID

I WAS SO YOUNG

FULL OF WELL..CUM

CAN YOU FORGIVE THIS?

IT IS MY ONLY WISH...

Chapter 3

QUOTES

ONE DAY YOU WILL LOOK AROUND AND REALIZE THAT YOU FORGOT TO LOOK AROUND?

PLAY A SONG THAT SOMEONE LIKES... AND YOU WILL ALWAYS HAVE A PARTNER

LOVE IS EXACTLY WHAT IT WANTS TO BE AT TIMES AND AT OTHER TIMES IT IS WHAT IT NEEDS TO BE

MISSING YOU LEADS ME TO REMINISCE OF DAYS LONG GONE AND FORGOTTEN BY YOU ON PURPOSE

*ALL THAT GLITTERS MAY NOT BE
GOLD BUT...
DOES THAT MEAN THAT IT IS NOT
VALUABLE OR WORTH HAVING?*

*MOVING MOUNTAINS MAY BE
DIFFICULT SO ... YOU MIGHT TRY
CLIMBING*

ONLY TIME WILL TELL BUT WHAT WILL IT TELL YOU WHEN IT DOES TELL?

WHEN YOU SMILE BEWARE OF THE FACE THAT SMILES BACK... IT MAY BE THE CALM BEFORE THE STORM

JUST WHEN YOU THINK YOU ARE DONE...
YOU TAKE A LOOK AROUND AND
THERE IS SO MUCH MORE TO DO

IF IT FEELS AS IF YOU ARE GETTING NOWHERE WITHIN A RELATIONSHIP THEN MOST LIKELY...
THAT IS THE CASE.

KILLING MY INSIDES ALL NIGHT
INSTANTLY I NEED SLUMBER
SO SATISFIED WITH HIM
SEXING MY MIND, BODY, AND
SOUL

MIND BLOWING ORGASMS IN
MANY VERSES
EXTRATERRESTRIAL LIKE LOVING

NICE AND NASTY AS I WANT TO BE IRRESISTIBLE WHEN I SET MY EYES ON YOU..

MANY MAY ATTEMPT TO CAPTIVATE BUT CAN'T..ALL ATTEMPTS FUTILE BECAUSE OF YOU

TIME WAITS FOR NO MAN, BUT A WOMAN WILL WAIT A LIFETIME IF IT'S CLOSE TO HER HEART

ALL I REALLY WANT IS..

FOLLOW YOUR MIND BECAUSE
THE HEART PLAYS GAMES
SOMETIMES..
REAL TALK

REACH FOR THE STARS AND IF
THE CLOUDS SHOULD GET IN THE
WAY... MOVE THEM

THE MOST LOGICAL PERSON IN THE GROUP IS USUALLY THE CRAZIEST; THEY JUST HAVE YET TO REALIZE IT

AS HUMANS WE ARE GUILTY BY NATURE AND PROVEN INNOCENT BY OUR DEEDS (THINK)

ALL ABOUT ME BECAUSE NO ONE ELSE WILL BE

PEOPLE ALWAYS WANT WHAT
THEY ARE NOT WILLING TO GIVE

Š

TAKE TIME TO SMELL
THE ROSES BUT WATCH
THE SNAKES IN THE
GRASS...

Š

Poetic

Interviews

It is hot and humid outside on this day and the sidewalks seem to need some type of liquid gratification. There seems to be no relief in sight from the sun's punishment. The craving for a Nice cold beverage from the corner store called to me but as I glanced at the time on the wall I realized that it was almost time for my phone interview with **Mr. Controversy** himself...

Poet Ruque!

I had so many questions for him but I wanted to keep it simple. We immediately greeted each other as if we were long lost cousins with laughter and a quick joke or two.

Nima- So why does it seem as if you are extremely hard on women when it comes to your poetry?

Poet Ruque- I believe it seems that way because I am mirroring the flaws that no one wants to approach them on. I learned to stop showing love and bite them to show them that they no longer have an affect on me.

Nima- What makes you tick when you are writing?

Poet Ruque- If someone decides to say something unnecessary or ignorant it pushes me. If you don't like it then don't read it.

Nima- Do you ever get to the point where you don't want to pick up a pen again?

Poet Ruque- At times I have tried to put myself in this mode but the fan base is too strong.

Nima- Do you feel that the poetry community that you belong to supports its artists enough?

Poet Ruque- No, due to the division and lack of unity. Lets go Poets!!

Nima- If you could use one song in order to change the worlds for the better, what song would it be?

Poet Ruque- "Live Your Life" by **T.I. and RIHANNA**, due to the fact that everyone wants to live life according to others perspectives instead of their own. It's "your" life not your moms, ya pops, ya man, ya wife, no no no...Your Life!!Be content with you.

Nima- Give me one word to describe your writing

Poet Ruque- Pain..A lot of my stuff came from relationships. Pain, we get hurt worse but we channel our pain. Yes, pain is the word.

Nima- Do you feel as if you as an artist have a responsibility to your fans?

Poet Ruque- We have to open the minds of people. We can disagree but hear it out. It's a lot of pressure because we offer so much verbally. Our mindset is different. Don't slack or fall off. You owe your fans the best at all times. It's disrespectful to do any less. It's possible to go beyond your goal: and then make another one. They say it's impossible you set yourself up for failure. We speak it into existence.

Nima- Who do you admire as an artist?

Poet Ruque-I admire **Black Ice**. He has his own flow. It's different and a lot of folks try to imitate him. Now within my circle...**Nadira Norjahan, Sapphire Blue, Janelle T. Harvey, Damien Cooper, and Wynter Solstyce just to name a few.**

Nima- Do you have groupies?

Poet Ruque- I have had a debate with my girl on this topic..but now I have to say I think so.

Nima- Past or Present who would like to meet?

Poet Ruque- I would like to meet **Mr. Langston Hughes**. I did a project on him. I got into him and read his stuff. I understood it. Life ain't been no crystal stairs...I admire Jill Scott and I have even tweeted her but she doesn't tweet back.

Nima- In your own words what is the difference between poetry and spoken word?

Poet Ruque- Poetry is written and spoken word is a physical visualization. How you draw the crowd in. You get addicted to the crowd and seeing the reaction of the crowd.

Nima- Do you feel that some men get into poetry for sex?

Poet Ruque- I think its genius. It's like carrots to catch a rabbit. Rabbits are smart. Different carrots for different types of rabbits. It works. If you can't get your specific rabbit then carrots will do.

Nima- Have you ever felt nervous?

Poet Ruque- When I met **Nadira Nmjahan,** she went up and I was like what do I do after that? It was like someone let off an m16. Sometimes when guest come up and bless the mic I still feel it but I get up and do me.

Nima- Do you think that your listeners take you seriously?

Poet Ruque- I think that people enjoy tapping into my flow.

Nima- When did you start writing poetry?

Poet Ruque- It was a homework assignment for an English teacher. I wanted to be a rapper when I was about 11 years of age. I thought poetry was for people of the gay community.. I hated it because I didn't understand it. Once I understood it.. It was like love at first sight. The way women put their feelings together. First person I shared it with was the Principle. He called me to his office and said that I had some serious talent. It took off from there. I started watching Def Poetry Jam and I got addicted. I got hooked and it became a habit and I had to have it...

It was a beautiful day in the city of brotherly love and sisterly affection. The streets were filled with people going on their way and being busy. As I check my watch in anticipation of my very important phone call. This brother was so gracious to bless me with his time. He was my first interview and he didn't mind that I had no format and had never done this prior to today.

On the phone I have One of the admins from the Collective...

Mr. Damien Cooper-D.P.S. also known as Poetic Spark!

I know he can hear me through the phone shuffle my papers but he doesn't say a word. I am nervous but I give myself a quick pep talk..(ok calm down, be cool, relax).

I am nervous and he finally gives a laugh to let me know that all is alright. Meeting him in person prior to this interview I can imagine his warm smile. He has that smile that you get from your Brother when you finally get the right man and he approves.

Nima- So how old were you when you fell in love with poetry?

D.P.S.- I had a teacher in the 9th grade that had the same name as my mother so there was a connection from day one. She use to give us words and we would have 45 minutes to do the assignment. I realized that I would be finished within 10 minutes. She would come to me and tell me how good my writings were.

Nima- Is it safe to say that the torch was lit?
D.P.S- Yes, the torch was lit.

Nima- Do you have poetry groupies?

D.P.S- (Smiling) Yes, it's all love all day though.

Nima- Who would you like to meet within the worlds of poetry or spoken word?

D.P.S- Dr. Maya Angelo. I would love to have met her. I have been a fan of hers since high school.

Nima- Ok, so within the **FPC** name 3 people that you admire and why?

D.P.S- Jody Tru Story Austin. She has a heart that is unreal beautiful sister. She is just love. Alicia C. Cooper. She has that essence that everyday realness. She moves me. **Adrianne ThePen Bautista**. She makes you step your game up

Nima- What's the difference between poetry and spoken word from your point of view?

D.P.S.- Well I'm no expert but to me Poetry is a blueprint, it's restricted, it's formatted, it's the foundation. Spoken word is Realness, raw, expression. You can't format expression.

Nima- What type of advice do you have for anyone thinking about stepping into the world of poetry or spoken word?

D.P.S- Don't over think it. It's going to come out.

It's your heart song. There is no blueprint.

Along with being an admin on the Collective Team, Damien has finished two books with one in the works. He is also a ghost writer for some Gospel, Hip Hop, and R& B musicians.
As I begin to wrap up our session and prepare for the next and final question, he takes a deep breath and with a look of uncertainty and fulfillment all in one he says.

"I haven't gotten back to me. I don't want to be like everyone else. I'm afraid of not finding Dame..."

Nima- In the world of poetry how would you like to be remembered or what could you say about poetry?

D.P.S- Poetry saved my life it saved my life...

My anticipation is building as I am filled with excitement of knowing that in less than 5 minutes I will be exchanging words with a very intelligent brother from within my poetry circle. I am not sure if I should grab my dictionary or just let the conversation take shape. In the end, I voted for the latter of the two.

His voice is very soothing and familiar. He greeted me with the word "**Peace**" and that was all it took to put my worries to rest. I gathered my pen, pad and thoughts in an instant, attempting to prepare for an over the phone interview with an original Hip Hop Connoisseur/poet/spoken word artist, and author of **(THE BOOK OF BORN FREE...THE WISDOM OF LIVING RIGHT NOW)**-

Mr. Born Free.. Carlos Wharton.. affectionately known to some as Los.

Nima- So at what age did you realize that you had a gift for words?

Born- I can't remember but I was told that at the age of 5-6-7 I had the ability. I would listen and watch speeches of Dr. King, Malcolm X, The Last Poets, and Nikki Giovanni. They could mesmerize you with their flow. It was like eating a desert within a desert.

Nima- Name someone past or present that you would love to meet?

Born- I would love to have met **Gil Scott Heron**. He was laying out his issues and problems. He manifested it in a soulful way. He saw the ills of our community and felt them deeply. I would have loved to ask him what it was that he was trying to articulate and how I could help him? He loved so much and hurt so much, that is was sometimes painful to watch and listen to him, but I loved that brother and wish that he was able to conquer his demons.

As I sit and listen to him speak with such passion and conviction I can feel his love for humanity on a whole but a deeper love and pain presence for his own people. He reminds me of a poster of Black Men united walking side by side for freedom during the 1950's. He could also easily be the 2014 version of the statue of the thinking man in my opinion.

Nima- What do you think is the difference between spoken word and poetry?

Born- I love both poetry and spoken word. They both elevate and transport me to different worlds and dimensions. Reading a poem on the page is dope and very relaxing and deeply spiritual at times, but when you hear it dancing in the atmosphere powered by a human heart and soul, it flies into another world. Verbal expression gives it a more rounded and fuller experience, but sitting down and reading a poem can be very moving and intimate. So at the end of the day, I love them both.

Nima- What advice would you give someone that wants to pick up a pen and write?

Born- Don't judge yourself. Stop thinking about what others will think about you. Speak the truth regardless.

Nima- On a scale from 1-10, how would you rate yourself?

Born- I'm ok. I really don't rate myself, I could be better. I'm striving every day to be most honest and open in my expression. In my humble opinion, **Wise Intelligent from the Legendary Poor Righteous Teacher** is the ill-est lyricist period! He's my brother and he makes me better and sharper.

Nima- At what age were you when you said your first rhyme?

Born- I was 10 years old. I had a notebook of rhymes. I had a lot of comic books and books of random people's thoughts and meditations. I loved watching a lot of television and Star Wars really pulled me in. It had an Epic quality and I love the battle between good in evil that was playing out within Luke. I believe that I'm a Jedi Knight and that's how I approach my rhymes and quotes.

Nima- Wow so you were a constant reader?

Born- Until girls came along I was heavy into books but I lost my library card on the down stroke.

Nima- So how do you feel about the poets in your circle?

Born- I believe that all of us have a divine talent and I enjoy everybody's light.

Nima- Do you feel like as an artist you have a responsibility to anyone?

Born- I feel as though as an artist you have a responsibility to raise the value of your direct community and the world in general. Not to say that everything has to be all deep and profound, but it does have to be honest. One of the issues in rap is that this is a lack of honesty and balance. The mainstream is too top heavy with the party and bullshit flow. They forgot that life isn't all about money, hoes, and clothes. Rap music and Hip Hop culture was created to stop the violence. It was designed to give our children a high self-esteem and an enhanced racial pride. So I'm just attempting to help redirect the focus and bring balance to the Soul Sonic Force!

Nima- Wow!

Born- All the BS isn't relevant...we're at a critical time in world history and if your lyrics and music don't help advance us and lift us up higher, please keep it moving!

Nima- When days have turned into years how would you like to be remembered?

Born- As a man who loved and cared deeply about his community. I want people to remember that I showed and proved my love and devotion through my ways and actions and not just with my words. I want them to remember that I told the truth. I want to inspire the youth. I am an activist. As an activist I must leave my community in a better condition than when I found it.

Nima- As I thank him for his time and patience during this phone conversation I can't help to listen to his voice that screams of a New York Hip Hop Head.

We talk some more and somewhere during our conversation I become so engulfed and captivated by his mind that I forget that I was doing an interview. His mind is as vast as the ocean.

We Mourn

In the time it took to put the finishing touches on this interview, the world has unfortunately lost some Iconic figures. The loss of **Nelson Mandela, Maya Angelou, and Ruby Dee**.
Though the world mourns the loss of these beautiful, trailblazing, talented, freedom fighting Icons, none will feel the loss as deeply as the African American community because they belonged to us lovingly. I had the opportunity to get **Mr. Wharton's** feelings on these tragic events. He spoke of these individuals with such passion and love. It was clear to see that he felt the loss on an entirely different level. It was as if he woke up each day and had breakfast with them and could no longer sit at the table without their presence.

I thanked him for the interview and in his low New York accent he said, **"Peace.."**

Since this interview I have added the terminology...(Its All Good-Peace-and Queen to my daily vocabulary) Thank You Born..

Peace

About The Author

Nima...

Born and raised in Philadelphia PA, has enjoyed reading and writing poetry and short stories since early childhood.She would learn to use her imagination and creativity to escape or break from the world around her.

Over time, she would learn to pull words and emotion from the same world she tried to escape. Through tragedy, pain, love, life, and lessons, she continues to write until she spills all of her ink or until she has nothing more to say.

With the love and support of her family, she will continue to grow and give all something to talk about.

Interview Disclaimer

All information was willingly given to the alias known as Nima Shiningstar-El to be used in her up coming book of poetry and/or fictitious urban novels.

All participants are under no contracts or duress during these interviews and have given Nima Shiningstar-El full permission to use their Pen Names as well as real names in her books

They are aware that no financial obligation will be on the part of Nima Shiningstar-El or her Estate regardless of financial gains in the future whether, by way of books, movies, music, etc.

I am releasing this information to the person that I know to be Nima Shiningstar-El or any other names that she has or will go by in the future or anyone she names as agent and/or Publisher in the future (BlaqRayn Publishing).

www.ingramcontent.com/pod-product-compliance
Lightning Source LLC
Chambersburg PA
CBHW031957040426
42448CB00006B/390